Guide to Wild DINOSAURS

Adam Yates
Illustrated by Jon Hughes

Sterling Publishing Co., Inc.
New York

Library of Congress Cataloging-in-Publication Data Avail

10 9 8 7 6 5 4 3 2 1

Published in 2002 by Sterling Publishing Co., Inc.
387 Park Avenue South, New York, NY 10016

First publsihed in Great Britain in 2002 by Collins, an imprin
Harper Collins *Publishers* Ltd.
Fulham Palace Road, London, W6 8JB

Distributed in Canada by Sterling Publishing
c/o Canadian Manda Group, One Atlantic Avenue , Suite 105
Toronto, Ontario, Canada M6K 3E7

Printed in Hong Kong

Sterling ISBN 0-8069-9346-4

IOW TO USE THIS BOOK

'his book covers 120 genera of dinosaurs and other ehistoric animals that lived alongside them (a genus ompasses a group of closely related species). They are ouped into three sections, each covering animals from a fferent period of the Mesozoic Era. Within each period the imals are organized according to the evolutionary relationships.

A symbol corresponding to those on the diagrams in this tion depict each major group. They are presented in the left-hand corner of each account so that you may see at a nce which group each animal belongs to. You can also see ckly which period each animal comes from by looking at e color-coded symbols: Yellow = Triassic, Green = Jurassic, rple = Cretaceous.

To show exactly when each creature lived, a time-wheel is en. Each one starts at the beginning of the Triassic 12 lock position and moves clockwise around the circle until finishes with the end of the Cretaceous at the 12 o'clock sition. The sector that is filled in red represents the time n in which that particular animal existed.

A "fact file" on each animal will give you basic information a glance. The classification gives you the list of evolutionary oups or "clades" that the animal belongs to, starting with the gest clade (Saurischia or Ornithichia for dinosaurs) and nding with the smallest non-family clade. A family is a clade f closely-related genera. The family name is given at the top each account above the name of each animal (which ppears in large type).

HAT IS A DINOSAUR?

many people a dinosaur is any large extinct animal, but to aeontologists, scientists who specialize in studying historic life, the name has a more precise meaning. Many mals that are commonly thought to be dinosaurs, such as g pterosaurs and swimming plesiosaurs, are not proper aurs, while modern birds are actually a surviving part of the dinosaur clan. The modern concept of the group Dinosauria is that it is a "real" branch of the reptile family tree. It is "real" in the sense that all dinosaurs are more closely related to one another than they are to any other reptile group. In other words, they are all descended from a single ancestral species: the first dinosaur. All descendants of this common ancestor are included in the Dinosauria, no matter how much they have changed during the course of their evolution. Such evolutionary groups, which include all descendants of a common ancestor, are called "clades," and it is a requirement of modern classifications of living things that all groups be clades. How does one identify an animal as a member of the clade Dinosauria? We look to the evolutionary novelties, or "derived characteristics" that the animal displays. We can assume that the ancestor of a clade had evolved some characteristics that were new to it and that its subsequent descendants inherited these derived characteristics (although it is possible for them to be erased or modified by subsequent evolution). In the case of dinosaurs, there are many rather technical features. Four of the most significant are listed below:

i). Special pairs of crests on the top of each neck vertebra that are used for the attachments of tendons to hold the neck in shape.

ii). A first finger, or thumb, that moves in a different direction to the other fingers; so when it is flexed, it moves across the palm and when it is extended, it points away from the other fingers. This allows the hand to grasp when the thumb is flexed, and also allows the large thumb claw to be used as a weapon when the thumb is extended.

iii). An asymmetrical hand with very small fourth and fifth fingers (the "ring" and "little" fingers, respectively).

iv). An interlocking and immobile joint between the main bone of the ankle and the larger of the two lower leg bones, making a stiffer, hinge-like ankle that can only bend in one direction of movement.

THE DINOSAURS' PLACE IN THE TREE OF LIFE

Due to the ever-branching nature of evolution, all clades (except the clade of all life) are nested inside larger clades, rather like Russian dolls. Dinosaurs are one clade among many (including our own) that are included in the great clade Vertebrata (animals with a backbone). Among the vertebrates they belong to the clade Tetrapoda (four-footed, mostly terrestrial vertebrates). Most animals figured in this book are tetrapods (the exception is *Hybodus*, a cartilaginous fish). Within the Tetrapoda, dinosaurs belong to the clade Amniota, which all share the derived character of an egg that contains a membrane surrounding the developing embryo.

The other tetrapod clade is the Amphibia, which have naked jelly-like eggs that are usually laid in water. The Amniota contains two large clades, the Synapsida and the Reptilia.

The Synapsida, which includes modern mammals, share the derived character of a single large hole in the skull for the attachment of jaw muscles. More advanced synapsids, of the Therapsida, also developed differentiated teeth (eg. incisors, canines, and molars) and a faster, "warm-blooded" metabolism.

The Reptilia share such derived characters as a dry scaly skin and excretion that involves uric acid (this reduces water loss during urination). Thus, they are well adapted for coping with hot, dry conditions.

Within the reptiles the largest clade is the Diapsida, which have two holes in the temporal region of their skull. Turtles are the only living reptiles that are not diapsids. The three main diapsid clades featured in this book are the Ichthyosauria, the Plesiosauria, and the Archosauria. Ichthyosaurs are superficially fish-like marine reptiles whose relationships to other diapsids are uncertain. Plesiosaurians are also marine reptiles that have lost the lower of the two temporal holes in the skull. They are more closely related to modern snakes and lizards than they are to Archosaurs.

The last clade, Archosauria or "ruling reptiles," contains crocodiles, pterosaurs (flying reptiles), dinosaurs, and birds (feathery flying reptiles). Archosaurs share the derived character of a large hole on each side of the skull, in front of each eye, and teeth that are set in sockets. Within the Archosauria, those that are more closely related to Crocodiles than to dinosaurs form a clade called Crurotarsi. Crurotarsans share an advanced swivel joint between the bones of the ankle.

Pterosaurs are more closely related to dinosaurs than to crocodiles, so they are placed in a clade called Ornithodira. All these relationships can be summed up in the following diagram of relationships, known as a cladogram.

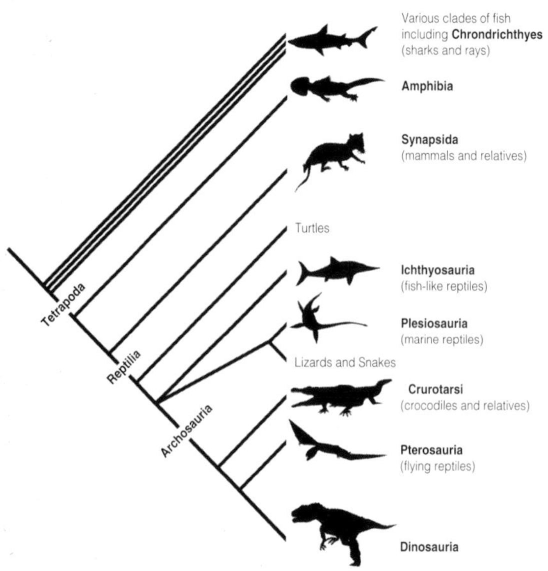

THE MAIN GROUPS OF DINOSAURS

All dinosaurs belong to one of two large clades, the Ornithischia ("Bird Hips") and the Saurischia ("Lizard Hips"). Ornithischians share two main derived characters: a bird-hipped pelvis and a toothless bone (called a predentary) in front of the lower jaws. The bird-hipped condition refers to the fact that the left and right pubis bones (bones in the front of the pelvis) have separated from each other and are rotated backwards to lie parallel to the ischia (bones from the back of the pelvis). This allowed the guts to move back under the hind legs so that they could become longer and heavier without making the animal front-heavy.

The predentary bone provided a stable, single-piece platform to support a horny beak. Both features are adaptations to a diet of plants, and all ornithischians were herbivores. The two main clades within Ornithischia were the Thyreophora ("shield bearers") and the Neornithischia ("new bird hips").

Thyreophorans were heavy-bodied quadrupeds that were armored with bony plates set into their skin. The group includes Stegosauria ("roofed lizards") that had a double row of very tall plates and spikes on either side of the midline and Ankylosauria ("fused lizards") that were squat, heavily armored forms with armor plating on their skulls.

Neornithischia shared the derived characters of a toothless gap in front of the main row of cheek teeth, and teeth that had a thicker layer of enamel on one side (so that a cutting edge was formed when the teeth were worn). Neornithischia itself is comprised of two large clades, the Marginocephalia and the Ornithopoda. Marginocephalians include the horned dinosaurs and the dome-headed dinosaurs. They were a diverse group that are united by a shelf of bone at the back of their heads. Ornithopods were a group of mostly bipedal herbivores that evolved some quadrupedal forms late in the Cretaceous period (see below).

Saurischians, for the most part, retain the primitive condition of having a pubic bone that pointed forward ("lizard-hipped" condition), but also share some advanced features, such as an elongated neck and extra joints between the vertebrae of the back (thus stiffening the trunk), that identify the group as a clade. Saurischia is made up of two clades containing rather different looking animals. One clade, the Sauropodomorpha, primarily consists of large, quadrupedal herbivores, whereas the other clade, the Theropoda, are entirely bipedal and are mostly carnivorous. Two groups are recognized within the Sauropodomorpha, although one might not be a clade.

The Sauropoda are definitely a clade and all share a gigantic body size, columnar, elephantine legs, and a tiny head. The

Prosauropoda include smaller, less specialized forms that may, or may not, be ancestral to the true sauropods.

Theropods are a clade that share a wishbone in the shoulder girdle and an extra joint in the middle of their lower jaws that allowed their jaws to clamp around struggling prey. The two main theropod clades are the Ceratosauria and Tetanurae. Ceratosaurs flourished early in the history of the dinosaurs, but some survived until the end of the Cretaceous. Ceratosaurs share the derived characteristic of fusing up many of the bones in their hips and feet. Tetanurans have a stiff tip to their tails and have only three fingers on each hand. Most tetanurans fall into one of two clades: the Carnosauria or the Coelurosauria.

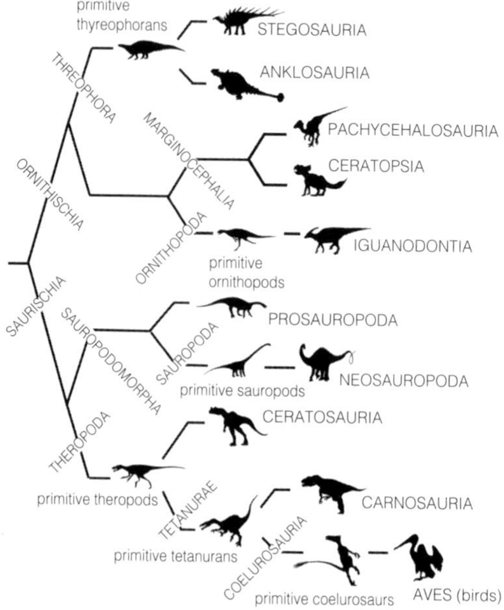

Carnosaurs were large, fierce predators with large heads and small arms. They share special pneumatic holes in the bones of the snout which identifies the group as a clade. Coelurosaurs, on the other hand, were small, lightly built animals with small heads and long arms (although exceptions, such as tyrannosaurids, did evolve). Advanced coelurosaurs share a number of characteristics with birds such as a large half-moon shaped bone in the wrist and a pubic bone that is bent backwards (as in ornithischians) that show that birds are a part of this clade. A number of coelurosaurian groups abandoned the predatory way of life and evolved into herbivores.

WHEN DINOSAURS LIVED

To discuss the Earth's immensely long history, geologists divide the past up into large chunks of time called "eras." These Eras are subdivided into smaller lengths called "periods." The Era that concerns us is the Mesozoic Era (245–65 million years ago). It is subdivided into three periods, the Triassic (245–208 million years ago), Jurassic (208–146 million years ago), and Cretaceous (146–65 million years ago).

The earliest known dinosaurs are about 230 million years old (from the Late Triassic Period). At that time there were only a few rare species. Synapsids and different groups of reptiles dominated the land. Nevertheless, by the end of the Triassic (210 million years ago) almost all medium- to large-sized land animals were dinosaurs. This dominance continued until the end of the Mesozoic Era (at the end of the Cretaceous Period, 65 million years ago). At this boundary, nearly all groups of dinosaur went extinct, but one small group of coelurosaurian theropods, the birds, did survive.

"WARM-BLOODED" OR "COLD-BLOODED" DINOSAURS?

Modern reptiles have a physiology that is commonly referred to as "cold-blooded." This is a poor term to use as it is both inaccurate (the body temperature of reptiles can be as high, or higher, than a similar-sized "warm-blooded" animal) and confuses more than one characteristic. Firstly, animals can be either endothermic or ectothermic. Endotherms generate their own heat internally by "burning" more food, while ectotherms rely on the sun to warm them up. Secondly, animals can be either homeothermic or poikilothermic.

Homeotherms have a constant body temperature whereas the body temperature of poikilotherms varies widely. Modern reptiles, except birds, ("cold-bloods") are mostly ectothermic and poikilothermic, but some are ectothermic homeotherms. Modern birds and mammals ("warm-bloods") are mostly endothermic and homeothermic, but some are endothermic poikilotherms. Reptiles, except birds, are more efficient than birds and mammals, as they need less food to live, but they become inactive when it is cold. Birds and mammals are, on the other hand, always ready for action, which is just as well because they have a metabolic furnace that needs constant fuelling.

The debate over which strategy the non-birdy dinosaurs used has gone on for more than two decades and is still not resolved. Most agree that dinosaurs were active for most of their lives and maintained a high degree of homeothermy, but many do not believe they achieved this by being endothermic.

FURTHER READING

There are a great many books dealing with the subject of dinosaurs and prehistoric life, some much better than others. Here is a brief—and by no means complete list—of the better titles:

Benton, M. J. 2000, *Vertebrate Palaeontology* (2nd edition). Blackwell Scientific, Oxford. The standard vertebrate palaeontology textbook. A good introduction to the broader aspects of prehistoric vertebrate life.

Currie, P. J. and Padian, K. (Eds) 1997. *Encyclopaedia of Dinosaurs*. Academic Press, San Diego. A collection of articles arranged alphabetically by leading experts. It is a large authoritative and comprehensive work, but the level of detail in the coverage is patchy.

Dingus, L. and Rowe, T. 1998. *The Mistaken Extinction:*

Dinosaur Evolution and the Origin of Birds. W. H. Freeman and Co., New York. An excellent introductory text into the modern methods of determining evolutionary relationships and biological classification. The best popular account of why birds should be classified as dinosaurs and an up-to-date account of dinosaur extinction.

Farlow, J. O. and Brett-Surman, M. K. (Eds) 1998. *The Complete Dinosaur*. Indiana University Press, Bloomington. A collection of articles by leading experts covering all aspects of dinosaur biology and evolution. One of the best all-around books for the dinosaur enthusiast.

Fatstovsky, D. E. and Weishampel, D. B. 1996. *The Evolution and Extinction of the Dinosaurs*. Cambridge University Press, Cambridge. The best dinosaur textbook.

Glut, D. 1997. *Dinosaurs: The Encyclopaedia*. McFarland and Co. Inc., Jefferson. A compendium of all the dinosaur genera that were known at the time of printing. Since the rate of discovery of new dinosaurs is so great, two supplementary volumes have been published since the original with more planned for the future. The only easily accessible place to find simple accounts and illustrations of the more obscure dinosaur genera.

Norman, D. B. 1985. *The Illustrated Encyclopaedia of Dinosaurs*. Salamander, London. The classic popular dinosaur book. Beautifully illustrated but unfortunately it is a little out of date now.

Weishampel, D. B., Dodson, P. and Osmólska, H. (Eds) 1990. *The Dinosauria*. University of California Press, Berkeley. The "bible" for serious dinosaur students. It is a technical account of the anatomy and classification of the major dinosaur groups with smaller sections on other aspects of dinosaur biology.

Wellnhofer, P. 1991. *The Illustrated Encyclopaedia of Pterosaurs*. Salamander, London. A companion volume to Norman's book. The only popular book devoted to pterosaurs, which is also lavishly illustrated.

ID FACT FILE

LENGTH:
8 ft (2.5 m)

WEIGHT:
55 lb (25 kg)

TIME:
Late Triassic

CLASSIFICATION:
Saurischia, Sauropodomorpha, Prosauropoda

DESCRIPTION:
Small, lightly built biped, with some ability to walk on all fours. Head small and neck short (compared to other prosauropods).

DIET:
Probably omnivorous, soft plants, and small animals.

Triassic
248–206 million yrs.

Jurassic
206–144 million yrs.

Cretaceous
144–65 million yrs.

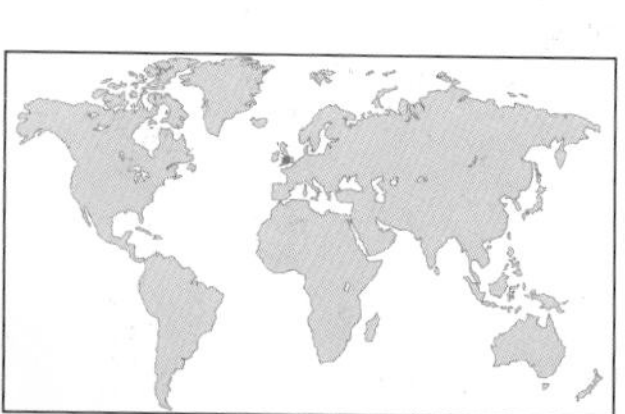

Thecodontosaurus

(socket-toothed lizard)

This was the first prosauropod dinosaur to be discovered. Its bones were found in sediments that fill ancient caves that were once a part of small, arid, islands in a shallow sea, in what is now south-west England.

Thecodontosaurus is also one of the most primitive of known prosauropods. Unlike its relatives, it was small and lightly built and could probably progress comfortably on two legs for much of the time.

It was not adapted for chewing a large amount of plant material, but neither was it fully adapted for life as a carnivore. Its teeth resembled those of a modern iguana, being leaf-shaped and coarsely serrated. This suggests that *Thecodontosaurus*, like the iguana, did include some plant material in its diet. In all probability it was an omnivore, eating both plants and small animals. Its thumb bore a defensive claw that was smaller than that of other prosauropods.

Unfortunately, many of the best *Thecodontosaurus* fossils were destroyed during World War II. However, since then bones have been found at a number of sites, which has allowed research to continue.

ID FACT FILE

LENGTH:
30 ft (9 m)

WEIGHT:
3 tons

TIME:
Late Triassic

CLASSIFICATION:
Saurischia, Sauropodomorpha, Prosauropoda

DESCRIPTION:
Moderately large, heavy bodied quadruped with short forelegs. Head small, with a pointed snout, placed on a moderately long neck.

DIET:
Herbivorous

Riojasaurus

(lizard from La Rioja)

Riojasaurus is a South American example of the melanorosaurid family. These were large, robust prosauropods that some scientists think may have been closely related to the ancestors of the gigantic sauropod dinosaurs. Other melanorosaurids have been found in Europe and South Africa.

Riojasaurus had a long, pointed snout, which may have been tipped with a small horny beak that would have helped it crop vegetation.

Triassic
248–206 million yrs.

Jurassic
206–144 million yrs.

Cretaceous
144–65 million yrs.

Its neck was long, but it was still quite stout when compared to other prosauropods such as *Plateosaurus* (see pp. 16–17). Like other prosauropods, it had a grasping, five-fingered hand and a four-toed foot. The hands would have been used when the animal reared up to feed on high branches. Its thumb was tipped with a large, curved claw that was used as a weapon. Because its body was so long and heavy, it would have had to walk upon all four limbs.

ID FACT FILE

LENGTH:
24½ ft (7.5 m)

WEIGHT:
1.5 tons

TIME:
Late Triassic

CLASSIFICATION:
Saurischia, Sauropodomorpha, Prosauropoda

DESCRIPTION:
Moderately large, heavy bodied quadruped with short forelegs. Head small, with a deep snout, on a long neck.

DIET:
Herbivorous

Plateosaurus

(flat lizard)

Plateosaurus was a typical prosauropod. It was also one of the most common Triassic dinosaurs and is known from dozens of sites across Europe. It has even been found as far away as Greenland. It is probable that so many skeletons are found because of the seasonally dry climate in which the animal lived.

During times of drought, many *Plateosaurus* became caught, and died, in the deep mud

Triassic
248–206 million yrs.

Jurassic
206–144 million yrs.

Cretaceous
144–65 million yrs.

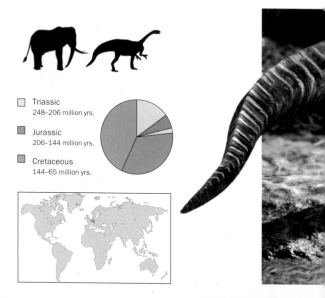

surrounding its waterholes. These skeletons would later be buried by sand brought by floodwaters when the drought broke.

Like most saurapodomorphs, *Plateosaurus* had a very large nasal chamber. The reason for this big nose is not known; it may have improved its sense of smell, or helped warm the air it breathed in. *Plateosaurus* differs from more primitive prosauropods by having jaws that were better designed to cope with chewing plants and by having a longer, thinner neck. It also had a strong "twist" to its thumb so that when it was straightened, its big claw would point away from the rest of the hand.

Mussaurus

(mouse lizard)

ID FACT FILE

Length:
8 in (20 cm) (baby)

Time:
Late Triassic

Classification:
Saurischia, Sauropodomorpha, Prosauropoda

Description:
Hatchlings were tiny, slender-limbed quadrupeds. Head short and deep. Lower jaw with a distinct "chin." Neck short for a prosauropod.

Diet:
Herbivorous

Mussaurus is mainly known from tiny skeletons of baby individuals. Adult prosauropod bones found nearby indicate they may have grown to 16 ft (5 m) in length. Several individuals were found close together, along with an egg that might belong to *Mussaurus*. Small though the skeletons were, they could not have fitted inside the egg. This is important because it suggests that the babies

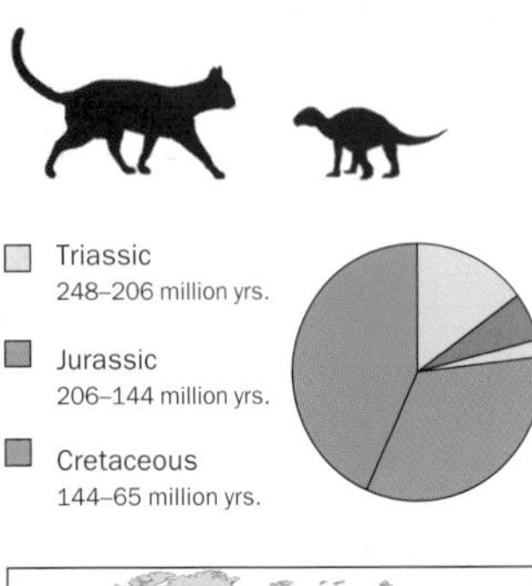

stayed in the nesting area long enough to outgrow their eggs. For this to happen, it is necessary for a parent to guard them and provide food. So perhaps *Mussaurus* had parental care, like a modern bird.

The skull of *Mussaurus* has some sauropod-like characteristics, such as a short, high skull and a chin. Does this mean the sauropods evolved their skulls by retaining juvenile features into adulthood, or is it just that *Mussaurus* is especially close to the ancestry of sauropods? Only the study of an adult *Mussaurus* will answer these questions.

ID FACT FILE

LENGTH:
13 ft (4 m)

WEIGHT:
770 lb (350 kg)

TIME:
Late Triassic

CLASSIFICATION:
Saurischia, Theropoda

DESCRIPTION:
Medium-sized, robust biped. Head large with short neck. Four fingered hands and four toed feet.

DIET:
Carnivorous, reptiles including other dinosaurs.

Herrerasaurus

(Herrera's lizard)

Herrerasaurus is one of the earliest known dinosaurus and was the largest one of its time. Scientists are divided in their opinion of its relationships. Some think it was a primitive saurischian that was related to the ancestor of both sauropodomorph and theropod dinosaurs while others think it was an early theropod.

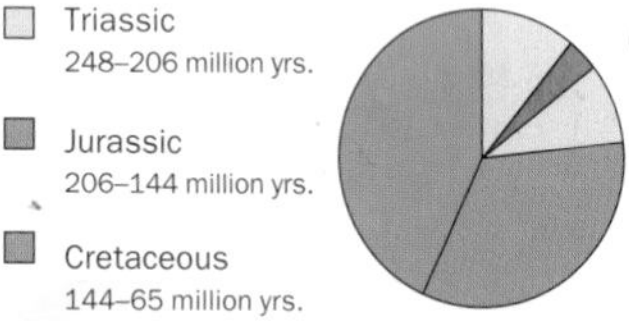

Triassic
248–206 million yrs.

Jurassic
206–144 million yrs.

Cretaceous
144–65 million yrs.

Like theropods, it was a bipedal predator; but unlike all other theropods, its first (big) toe was not reduced and the third (middle) finger was the longest. Its hands were well adapted for grasping and bore sharp, curved claws. It also had a large, deep skull armed with large sharp teeth. The middle teeth of the upper jaw were especially large and formed "fangs" that would have stuck out from underneath its lips. However, its legs did not have the proportions of a fast runner, so it may have ambushed its prey.

ID FACT FILE

LENGTH:
10 ft (3 m)

WEIGHT:
44 lb (20 kg)

TIME:
Late Triassic

CLASSIFICATION:
Saurischia, Theropoda, Ceratosauria

DESCRIPTION:
Small lightly built biped. Head long and low on a long, slender neck. Hands with four fingers and feet with four toes.

DIET:
Carnivorous, reptiles, and amphibians.

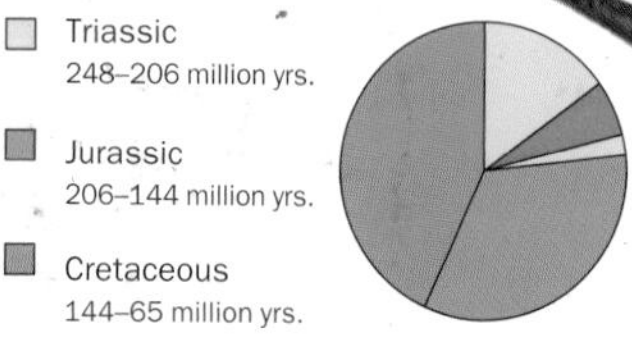

Coelophysis

(hollow form)

Coleophysis was a successful predator of the Late Triassic. A mass burial of hundreds of complete skeletons, found at Ghost Ranch in New Mexico, makes this one of the best known Triassic dinosaurs. These dinosaurs probably died together around a waterhole during a bad drought. The stomach contents of some of these skeletons show that *Coleophysis* was not above eating smaller members of its own species during times of hardship.

Triassic
248–206 million yrs.

Jurassic
206–144 million yrs.

Cretaceous
144–65 million yrs.

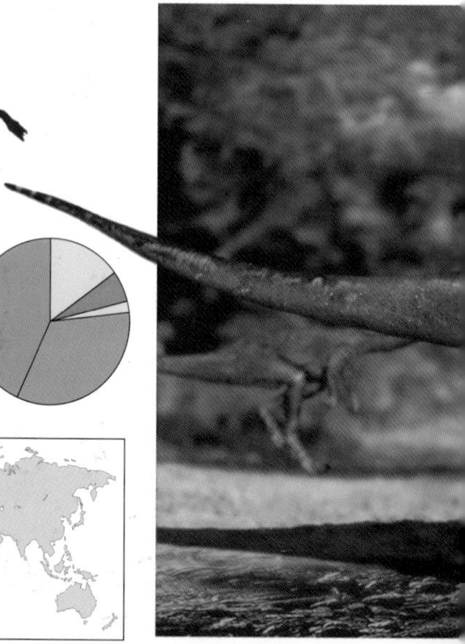

Coleophysis was more lightly built than the earlier *Herrerasaurus* (see pp. 20–21), so it would have been more nimble. Its foot also differed from that of *Herrerasaurus*, in that the first toe was reduced in size and its bones did not make contact with the ankle. This condition is also found in all later theropod dinosaurs including modern birds. *Coleophysis* and its closest relatives also had a peculiar notch in the upper jaw, just below the nostril. The function of this notch is unknown.

Although quite slender, *Coleophysis* had large, sharp serrated teeth and may have been able to take quite large prey, especially it it hunted in groups.

ID FACT FILE

LENGTH:
17 ft (20 kg)

TIME:
Late Triassic–Early Jurassic.

CLASSIFICATION:
Saurischia, Theropoda, Ceratosauria

DESCRIPTION:
Medium-sized lightly built biped. Like *Coelophysis* only larger.

DIET:
Carnivorous, maybe *Plateosaurus*.

Liliensternus

(named after Count Von Lilienstern)

This animal was a European relative of *Coleophysis* (see pp. 22–23). The main difference being that it was larger and had fewer vertebrae taking part in the connection between the spine and the hip girdle. Like *Coleophysis,* it had a slender build and a distinctive notch in the upper jaw.

For many years the bones of this animal were plastered into the wall of a privately owned castle in Germany. They now

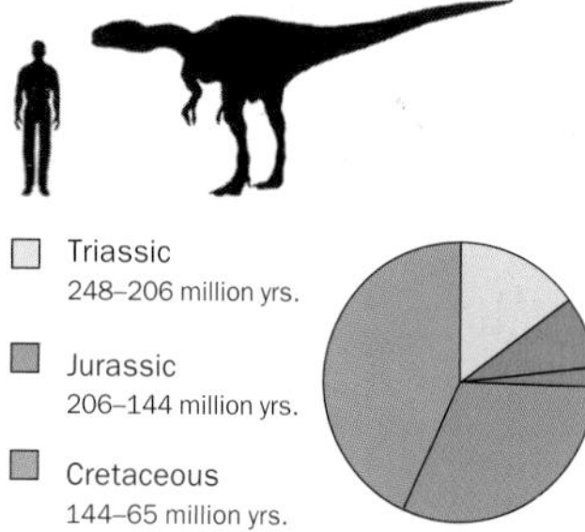

reside in the Humboldt Museum of Natural History in Germany and can be studied properly. Bones of a second species of *Liliensternus* have been found in France. This species was slightly younger than the original German one and lived during the Early Jurassic. Few other dinosaur genera are known to cross the boundaries of geological periods.

The only known skull is badly broken, so it is not possible to tell whether *Liliensternus* had the twin crests often seen in early ceratosaurs (see *Dilophosaurus*, pp.66–67). *Liliensternus* had quite large teeth and may have hunted *Plateosaurus* (see pp. 16–17), the most common dinosaur that shared its habitat.

ID FACT FILE

LENGTH:
20 ft (6 m)

TIME:
Late Triassic

CLASSIFICATION:
Reptilia, Diapsida, Archosauria, Crurotarsi

DESCRIPTION:
Long, heavy-bodied quadruped. Skull large and deep, with large, sharp teeth. Neck short. Back and tail armored. Five fingers and toes.

DIET:
Carnivorous, reptiles, and amphibians.

Postosuchus

(crocodile from Post)

Originally reconstructed as a biped related to the ancestor of *Tyrannosaurus* (see pp. 196–197), we now know that *Postosuchus* was a quadruped more closely related to modern crocodiles than to any dinosaur. It was a large, fierce carnivore that probably filled the role of top predator in its environment.

It would be another 150 million years before any non-dinosaurian land animal would fill this role. *Postosuchus*, like dinosaurs, walked erect, with its body

Triassic
248–206 million yrs.

Jurassic
206–144 million yrs.

Cretaceous
144–65 million yrs.

lifted high off the ground and its limbs tucked underneath. This is quite an unusual posture among crocodile relatives (a group called the Crurotarsi), which usually have a more sprawling gait.

Like other crurotarsans, including modern crocodiles, *Postosuchus* was lightly armored with pairs of bony plates that extended along its back and tail. This would have have made it heavy, which means it is likely that *Postosuchus* was an ambush predator rather than a pursuit predator.

The footprints of *Postosuchus* and its relatives have been known for a long time, although at one time they were thought to be made by a giant frog!

ID FACT FILE

Length:
10 ft (3 m)

Time:
Late Triassic

Classification:
Reptilia, Diapsida, Archosauria, Crurotarsi

Description:
Long, low-slung, heavy bodied quadruped. Head small, ending in little pig-like snout. Heavily armored over the back and tail. Sides armored with short spikes. Five toes and fingers.

Diet:
Herbivorous, low growing plants, and tubers.

Stagonolepis

(drop scale)

Like *Postosuchus* (see pp. 26–27), *Stagonolepis* was an archosaur related to the ancestors of crocodiles, but it was a very different animal. Its most outstanding feature was its armor, which completely covered the back and tail in close fitting rectangular plates. These plates fitted together to form a jointed, flexible carapace.

Along each of its flanks was a row of short, stout spikes. Even the belly and

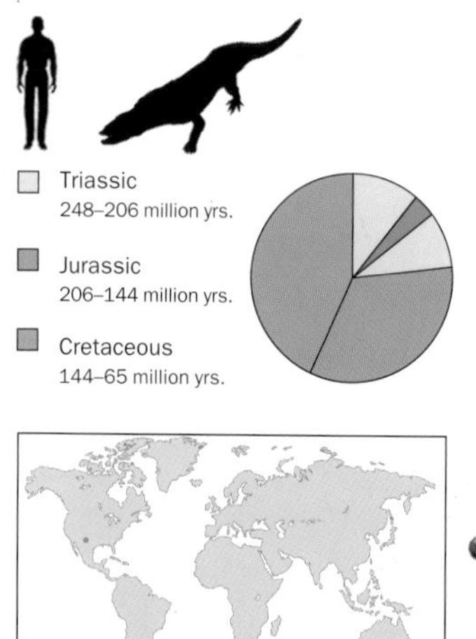

the underside of the tail were covered with bony plates. In other related species, these spikes became long, dangerous prongs that protected the flanks and shoulders. Its skull, with its toothless snout and small blunt teeth at the rear of the jaws, was also very different from the carnivorous archosaurs. The snout tip was blunt and upturned, looking a little like a pig.

It probably used its snout to grub through soft soil for roots and tubers. The body of *Stagonolepis* was rather narrow from side to side, but it had close relatives whose bodies grew very wide and flat. Combined with their armored carapace, these must have looked a lot like turtles.

ID FACT FILE

Length:
10 ft (3 m)

Weight:
1 ton

Time:
Late Triassic

Classification:
Synapsida,
Therapsida,
Dicynodontia

Description:
Heavy bodied quadruped with hippopotamus-like proportions. Head very large and neck short. Mouth with a horny beak and two tusks. Limbs stout and sprawling.

Diet:
Herbivorous, low browser.

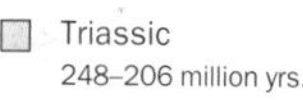
Triassic
248–206 million yrs.

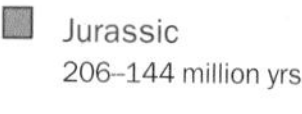
Jurassic
206–144 million yrs.

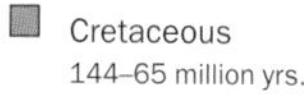
Cretaceous
144–65 million yrs.

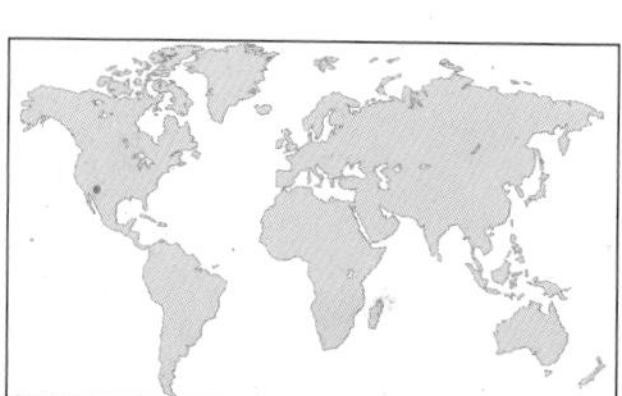

Placerias

(the pleasing one)

Placerias was one of the last dicynodonts, a successful group of herbivores that flourished earlier in the Triassic Period and in the Permian before that. The dicynodonts belonged to the Synapsida, a group of terrestrial vertebrates that includes mammals and their extinct relatives.

Although frequently called "mammal-like-reptiles," this is not strictly true and *Placerias* would have lacked such features as a dry scaly skin and uric

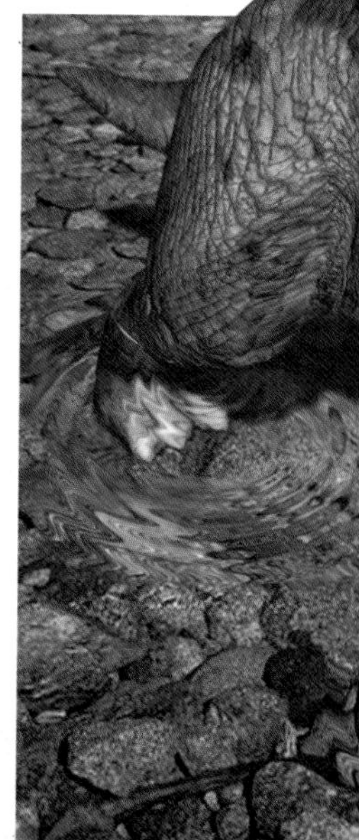

acid excretion that identify true reptiles. During their history, dicynodonts lost most of their teeth until only two remained. These formed a pair of small tusks in the upper jaw.

Some *Placerias*, perhaps the males, had large, bony spikes projecting down and out from the upper jaw. The front of the mouth formed a sharp beak that would have chopped its food into coarse pieces. It then relied on its massive gut, in its barrel-shaped body, to slowly ferment the food. Its limbs were short and squat and would have restricted it to a slow walking gait.

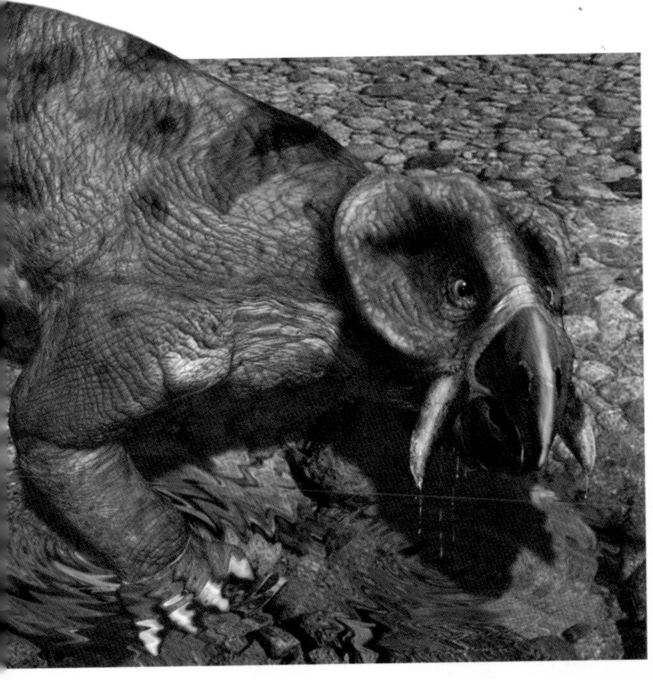

Scelidosaurus

(limb lizard)

ID FACT FILE

LENGTH:
11½ ft (3.5 m)

WEIGHT:
143 lb (65 kg)

TIME:
Early Jurassic

CLASSIFICATION:
Ornithischia, Thyreophora

DESCRIPTION:
Small, heavy-bodied quadruped. Head small and pointed. Mouth tipped with a small horny beak. Neck, back, flanks, and tail armored with longitudinal rows of bony studs set in the skin. Four hind toes, forefoot unknown.

DIET:
Herbivorous

Scelidosaurus is best known from the famous cliffs near Lyme Regis in England, where a number of skeletons have been found. These were buried in marine mudstones, suggesting that a river carried their carcasses out to sea before burial. Less complete remains are known from non-marine sediments in North America and China.

Scelidosaurus was a primitive member of the Thyreophora, a group of

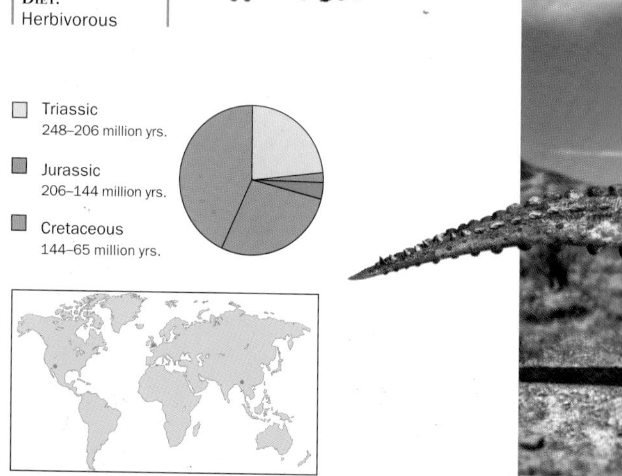

armored ornithischians that includes stegosaurs and ankylosaurs. Although *Scelidosaurus* was not a light biped, like the ancestral ornithischians, it had not developed the short, elephant-like feet of later thyreophorans either.

Its armor consisted of a double row of keeled studs, extending along its neck and back, with four additional rows on each of its flanks. The tail bore an upper and lower row of tall studs and a row of lower studs on each side. There was a unique pair of triple-spiked plates immediately behind the head.

ID FACT FILE

LENGTH:
13 ft (4 m)

WEIGHT:
660 lb (300 kg)

TIME:
Middle Jurassic

CLASSIFICATION:
Ornithischia, Thyreophora, Stegosauria

DESCRIPTION:
Medium-sized heavy bodied quadruped. Head small with a blunt snout. A double row of tall spike-like plates extending along the neck, back, and tail base. Two pairs of spikes at the tail tip, and a large pair over the shoulders.

DIET:
Herbivorous

Huayangosaurus

(lizard from Huayang)

Huayangosaurus is the most primitive known stegosaur. Unlike all others, the front of the upper beak bore a row of small teeth. It also had relatively long forelimbs so its back would not have sloped down towards the shoulders as it did in other stegosaurs. Along its sides was a single row of small, bony studs rather like those seen in *Scelidosaurus* (see pp. 32–33). Like all stegosaurs, the double row of armor along its neck, back, and

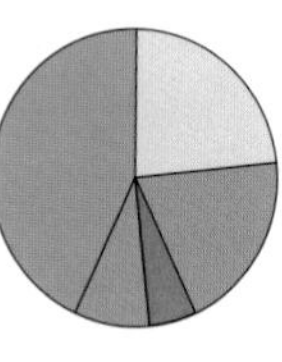

tail base was enlarged into a series of tall spikes and plates. In *Huayangosaurus* these were all quite narrow and pointed, although they did become broader and more plate-like towards the head.

Like all thyreophorans, it had small teeth with no effective chewing surface. These could only chop its food into coarse pieces, so it must have relied on large guts and high volumes of food to get the nourishment it required.

ID FACT FILE

LENGTH:
15 ft (4.5 m)

TIME:
Late Jurassic

CLASSIFICATION:
Ornithischia, Thyreophora, Stegosauria

DESCRIPTION:
Medium-sized quadruped, armored with a double row of tall armor plates that grade into spikes over the hips and tail.

DIET:
Herbivorous

Dacentrurus

(very spiky tail)

Dacenturus was the first stegosaur to be discovered. Its skeleton, which was found in 1874, had drifted out to sea before being buried in marine muds. It is distinctive in having forelimbs that are relatively longer than in other stegosaurids, though they were not as long as they were in *Huayangosaurus* (see pp. 34–35). It also had distinctively sharp front and back edges to its tail spines.

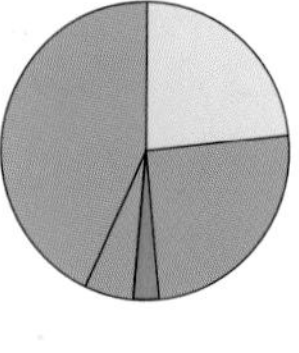

Apart from these features, it was a typical stegosaurid. The back and tail was armored with a double row of paired plates or spines.

Over the neck and shoulders, these were small oval plates, but became more elongated and spine-like as the row progressed towards the tail; so that by the hips, they were long spines. These spines continued along the length of the tail and reached lengths of more than 18 in (45 m).

ID FACT FILE

LENGTH:
16½ ft (5 m)

WEIGHT:
700 lb (320 kg)

TIME:
Late Jurassic

CLASSIFICATION:
Ornithischia, Thyreophora, Stegosauria

DESCRIPTION:
Medium-sized quadruped, with short forelimbs and a sloping back. Armored with a double row of tall armor plates grading into spikes over the hips and tail. Tail terminated with a pair of long spikes. A pair of spikes over the shoulders.

DIET:
Herbivorous

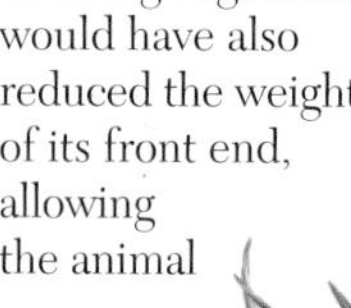

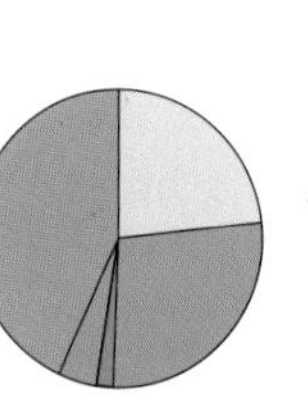

Kentrosaurus

(spiked lizard)

Kentrosaurus was a typical stegosaur. It had paired rectangular plates over the neck and shoulders that graded into pairs of sharp spikes over its hips and tail. An extra pair of spikes also guarded the shoulders. The forelimbs were particularly short compared to the hind limbs. This would have enabled it to browse on ground covering vegetation but would have also reduced the weight of its front end, allowing the animal

to rear up onto its hind legs to browse on trees. The tall spines of the vertebrae over its back and hips may have provided the necessary leverage to allow its back muscles pull it into the upright position.

Although the skull of *Kentrosaurus* is only known from fragments, it was apparently quite like that of *Stegosaurus*, which was long and low with a pointed snout and tipped with a toothless beak.

ID FACT FILE

Length:
30 ft (9 m)

Weight:
2.5 tons

Time:
Late Jurassic

Description:
Large-sized quadruped, with short forelimbs and a sloping back. Head small, beak long and narrow. Two alternating rows of large triangular plates over the back and hips. Tail tipped with two pairs of spikes.

Diet:
Herbivorous

Stegosaurus

(roofed lizard)

By the most famous and well-known stegosaur, *Stegosaurus* is actually quite unusual for the group. It was much larger and lacked the shoulder spines of the other stegosaurs. It also had a basket of little bony studs protecting its throat. Most obvious, however, was the gross enlargement of the dorsal armor into broad triangular plates, which gave the animal its distinctive profile. The arrangement of these plates has been the subject of controversy, but new and complete specimens show that the popular model of

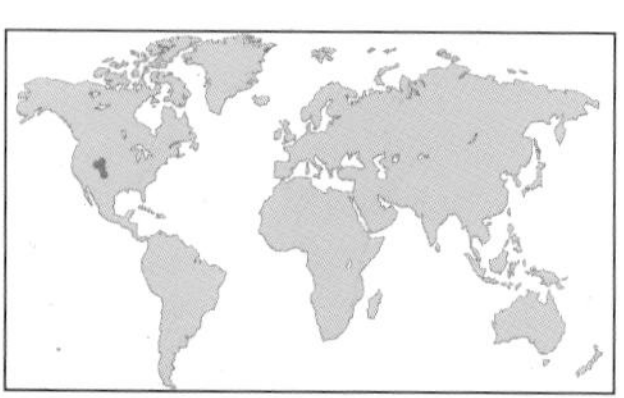

two alternating rows is correct. The function of these plates has been equally controversial. They could have been radiators for dumping excess heat, but this is unlikely because an insulating horny sheath probably covered them. Perhaps they were simply for display.

Like *Huayangosaurus* (see pp. 34–35), the two pairs of spikes on the end of the tail, when swung from side to side, would have made an effective weapon.

ID FACT FILE

LENGTH:
3 ft (1 m)

WEIGHT:
4½ lb (2 kg)

TIME:
Early Jurassic

CLASSIFICATION:
Ornithischia, Neornithischia, Ornithopoda.

DESCRIPTION:
Small-sized, lightly built quadruped, capable of bipedal locomotion. Head triangular with two pairs of large fangs. Five fingered hand with large thumbclaw. Four toed foot.

DIET:
Herbivorous, ground covering vegetation.

Heterodontosaurus

(different-toothed lizard)

Heterodontosaurus was an unusual little ornithischian. Currently classified as an ornithopod, it has a bony lump on each cheek, suggesting that it might be related to pachycephalosaurs and ceratopsians. Behind the typical beak of ornithischians, it had a pair of tusk-like teeth in both the upper and lower jaws. These tusks had fine serrations along their edges, which has led one palaeontologist to propose that *Heterodontosaurus* included some meat in its diet. The cheek teeth are very well adapted

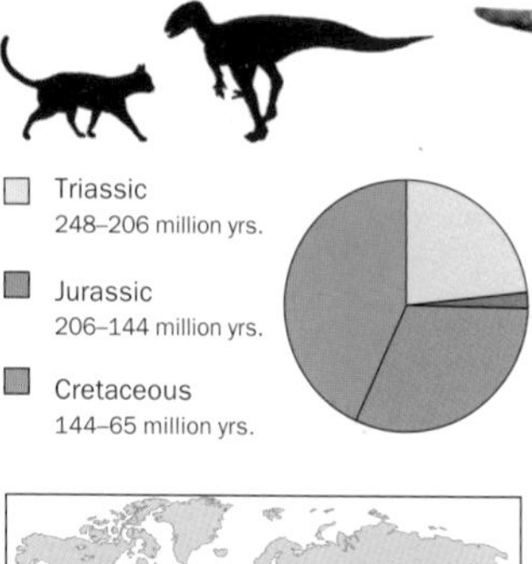

to chewing plants, so this species was unlikely to have been carnivorous. The tusks were probably used in display or defence.

Similar skulls have been found that do not have these tusks. They have been named as a separate genus, *Abrictosaurus*, but perhaps they are just female *Heterodontosaurus*. Although lightly built with short arms, like *Hypsilophodon* (see pp. 148–149), its vertebral column was bent sharply downwards at the front, which suggests that—for at least some of the time—it walked on all fours.

Dryosaurus

(oak lizard)

Dryosaurus looked very much like a larger version of *Hypsilophodon* (see pp. 148–149), but it possessed numerous specializations seen in more advanced ornithopods, which is why it is classified as an iguanodontian. These specializations include the loss of teeth from the front of the upper jaws; diamond-shaped teeth with strong, central ridges and deep grooves on the thigh-bone, just above the knee, for the passage of strong muscles.

ID FACT FILE

LENGTH:
13 ft (4 m)

WEIGHT:
220 lb (100 kg)

TIME:
Late Jurassic

CLASSIFICATION:
Ornithischia, Neornithischia, Ornithopoda, Iguanodontia

DESCRIPTION:
Medium-sized, lightly built, long-legged biped with a small, short skull. Arms short with four blunt-clawed fingers and feet with three toes.

DIET:
Herbivorous

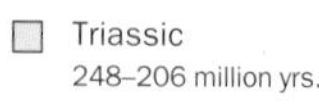

Triassic
248–206 million yrs.

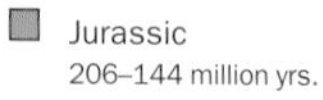

Jurassic
206–144 million yrs.

Cretaceous
144–65 million yrs.

Dryosaurus has been found in both Africa and North America. The species from these two continents are almost identical, giving powerful evidence that there was a continuous connection of land between them at the time.

The bone microstructure of *Dryosaurus* reveals that it grew quickly to adulthood without pausing. This means that either it was "warm-blooded," like a mammal, or that the climate in which it lived was equable for the entire year thus allowing such rapid and continuous growth.

ID FACT FILE

LENGTH:
23 ft (7 m)

WEIGHT:
600 lb (270 kg)

TIME:
Late Jurassic

CLASSIFICATION:
Ornithischia, Neornithischia, Ornithopoda, Iguanodontia

DESCRIPTION:
Medium-sized, heavily built biped with a long, low skull. Hands with five fingers and feet with four toes.

DIET:
Herbivorous

Camptosaurus

(bent lizard)

Camptosaurus was another early iguanodontian, like *Dryosaurus* (see pp. 44–45), but its larger, heavier body and long snout with close packed teeth were more like later, advanced, iguanodontians such as *Iguanodon* (see pp. 156–157).

Nevertheless, *Camptosaurus* retained a number of primitive features not seen in more advanced iguanodontians, such as fewer than 20 rows of teeth in each jaw, a

Triassic
248–206 million yrs.

Jurassic
206–144 million yrs.

Cretaceous
144–65 million yrs.

hand adapted to bearing weight while walking on four legs, and a small inner toe (equivalent of our "big toe"). Its teeth only had a tough enamel layer on one side, which formed a sharp cutting edge.

This feature is also found in later iguanodontians and indicates that they may have been including tougher browse in their diet, with more thorough chewing of their food. With its stockier body, *Camptosaurus* would not have been as swift as its contemporary, *Dryosaurus*.

ID FACT FILE

LENGTH:
13 ft (4 m)

WEIGHT:
330 lb (150 kg)

TIME:
Early Jurassic

CLASSIFICATION:
Saurischia
Sauropodomorpha
Prosauropoda

DESCRIPTION:
Like Plateosaurus, only smaller and with a larger thumb and claw.

DIET:
Herbivorous

Massospondylus

(massive spine)

Massospondylus was smaller, but otherwise similar in appearance to the Triassic *Plateosaurus* (see pp. 16–17). The differences between the two largely lie in details of the skull and teeth. The teeth of *Massospondylus* were peg-shaped and weakly serrated compared to the leaf-shaped, heavily serrated teeth of *Plateosaurus*.

Externally, the main difference would have been that *Massospondylus* had relatively bigger claws on the thumb and big toe.

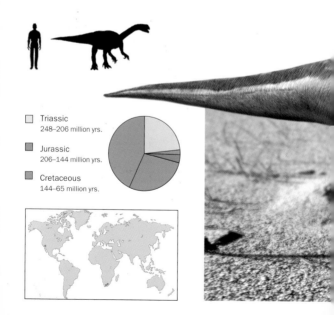

Triassic
248–206 million yrs.

Jurassic
206–144 million yrs.

Cretaceous
144–65 million yrs.

Massospondylus is interesting because its remains are commonly found in rocks that were once sand dunes in a desert. It shared these deserts with close relatives of *Coelophysis* (see pp. 22–23), which probably preyed upon it.

Deserts were widespread throughout the world in the Early Jurassic, and *Massospondylus* has been found in such far flung locations as Southern Africa and Western North America. Some palaeontologists have speculated that *Massospondylus* was a carnivore, but since it was the most common dinosaur in its habitat, this is unlikely—there would not have been enough prey in these desert areas to support large groups of *Massospondylus*.

ID FACT FILE

LENGTH:
23 ft (7 m)

TIME:
Early Jurassic

CLASSIFICATION:
Saurischia
Sauropodomorpha
Sauropoda

DESCRIPTION:
Large heavy-bodied quadruped. Limbs columnar. Foot with five toes, the first four with flat claws.

DIET:
Herbivorous

Vulcanodon

(volcano tooth)

Until recently this was the earliest and most primitive of known sauropods; however, new discoveries in China and Thailand may take these titles from it. The only known specimen was found sandwiched between lava flows, hence its name, which means "volcano tooth." The teeth that were found with the headless skeleton were blade-shaped and belonged to a carnivore. At first scientists thought that *Vulcanodon* may have been a carnivorous sauropod; however, its slow-moving, heavy body was most inappropriate for predation.

Triassic
248–206 million yrs.

Jurassic
206–144 million yrs.

Cretaceous
144–65 million yrs.

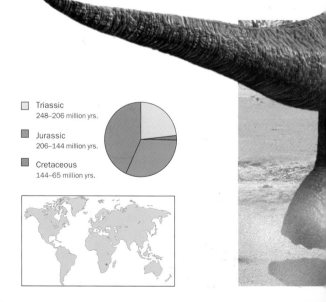

All of the teeth lacked roots and probably became mixed with the *Vulcanodon* remains when a carnivorous dinosaur fed on its carcass and shed some teeth. This was not the first time that such an association has fooled palaeontologists.

Vulcanodon shares columnar, elephantine limbs with more advanced sauropods, but did not have the short compact foot that these dinosaurs had. Instead, the foot of *Vulcanodon* was longer, like that of a prosauropod.

ID FACT FILE

LENGTH:
33 ft (10 m)

WEIGHT:
5 tons

TIME:
Middle Jurassic

CLASSIFICATION:
Saurischi
Sauropodomorpha
Sauropoda

DESCRIPTION:
Large heavy-bodied quadruped with a long neck and a small head. Hand with five short fingers, first with a large claw. Foot with five short toes, first three with claws. Long tail ending in a bony club with three conical spikes.

DIET:
Herbivorous

Shunosaurus

(lizard from Shuo)

Shunosaurus is one of the few sauropods known from its entire skeleton. Many specimens were unearthed by Chinese palaeontologists working in Dashanpu Quarry in the Sichuan province.

It was a primitive member of a uniquely Chinese family of sauropods, the Euhelopodidae. They were characterized by having greatly elongated necks. The neck of *Shunosaurus* was long (it had an extra vertebra compared to other early sauropods), but it was quite short compared to its advanced relatives such

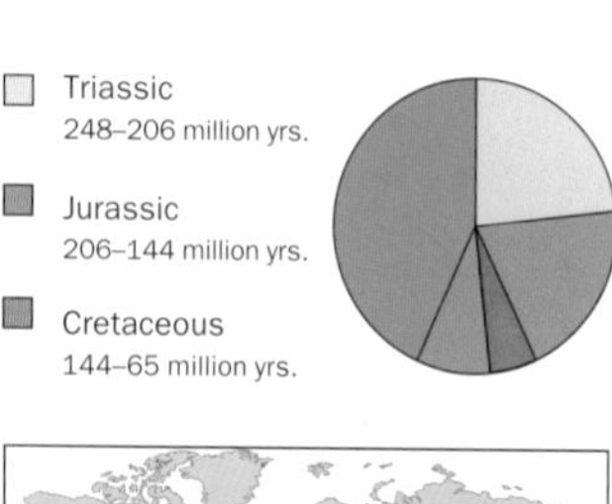

as *Mamenchisaurus* (see pp.54–55). The head of *Shunosaurus* was typical for an early sauropod, with broad U-shaped jaws filled with spoon-shaped teeth and large nostrils placed high up on the snout.

A unique feature of *Shunosaurus* was that its tail ended in a bony club with a row of conical spikes across the top. No other sauropod had such a weapon, which could have been used for defence against predators or territorial battles with other *Shunosaurus*.

Like other sauropods, *Shunosaurus* had a large claw on its thumb, which could have been used for defense or simply for gripping the ground.

ID FACT FILE

LENGTH:
75 ft (23 m)

WEIGHT:
18 tons

TIME:
Late Jurassic

CLASSIFICATION:
Saurischia
Sauropodomorpha
Sauropoda

DESCRIPTION:
Very large quadruped with an immensely long neck and a tiny head. The forelimbs were long and the back sloped down from the shoulders to the hips.

DIET:
Herbivorous

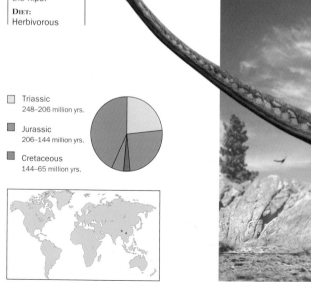

Triassic
248–206 million yrs.

Jurassic
206–144 million yrs.

Cretaceous
144–65 million yrs.

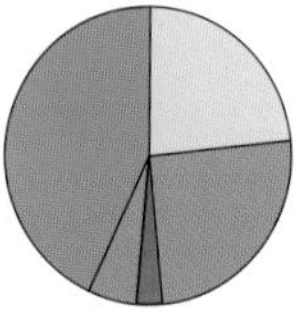

Mamenchisaurus

(lizard from Mamenchi)

Mamenchisaurus was an advanced relative of *Shunosaurus*. It had carried the neck elongation trend to its extreme, with seven extra vertebrae in its neck and the longest neck known in the animal kingdom (9.8 m/32 ft). Strangely, the neck may not have been able to be raised up, it instead gave the animal a greater feeding range while standing still since certain details of its skeleton resembled *Diplodocus* (see pp. 58–59) and its relatives, such as split spines on top of the trunk vertebrae and sled-like bones in the tail, so *Mamenchisaurus* was first classified as a diplodocid. However, when the skull of *Mamenchisaurus* was finally found, it turned out to be almost identical to that of *Shunosaurus* (see pp. 52–53).

We now know that *Mamenchisaurus* is not especially close to diplodocids and that the skeletal similarities between the two are the result of convergent evolution (similar pressures and problems producing similar adaptations in unrelated animals).

ID FACT FILE

LENGTH:
70 ft (21 m)

WEIGHT:
22.5 tons

TIME:
Late Jurassic

CLASSIFICATION:
Saurischia
Sauropodomorpha
Sauropoda
Neosauropoda

DESCRIPTION:
Very large heavy-bodied quadruped. Head small with long, low snout. Long, thick neck. Columnar limbs. Back sloped down to the shoulders. Single large claw on forefoot. Hindfoot with three claws. Tail ended in long whip-like tip.

DIET:
Herbivorous

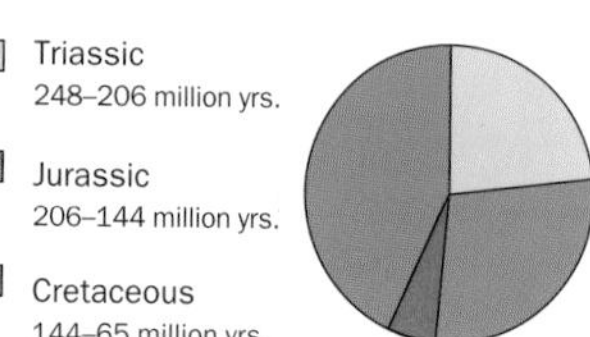

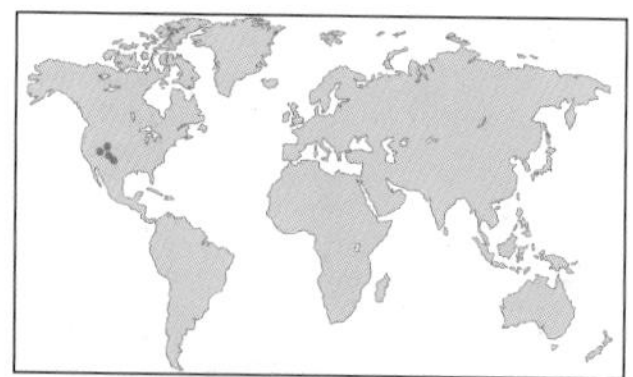

Apatosaurus

(deceptive lizard)

More commonly known in the popular press as *Brontosaurus*, this animal has been dogged by misunderstandings since it was first found in the American Midwest in the 1870s. When reconstructing the skeleton for the first time, its describer Othniel Marsh, used a skull that was found some distance from the original, headless skeleton. The skull closely resembled that of *Camarasaurus* (see pp. 62–63), which was supposed to be a relative.

As our understanding of sauropod anatomy improved, this reconstruction became an oddity.

Despite its thick limbs and heavy body, *Apatosaurus* shares many features with the light-weight, *Diplodocus* (see pp. 58–59). These include short forelimbs with a back that slopes up from the shoulders to the hips, sled-like bones in the tail, and a long whip-like tip to the tail. The puzzle was solved when the true skull of *Apatosaurus* was identified. It is almost identical to that of *Diplodocus*, and not at all like *Camarasaurus*, resulting in a reclassification of *Apatosaurus*.

ID FACT FILE

LENGTH:
90 ft (27 m)

WEIGHT:
19.5 tons

TIME:
Late Jurassic

CLASSIFICATION:
Saurischia
Sauropodomorpha
Sauropoda
Neosauropoda

DESCRIPTION:
Very large but slender quadruped. Head small with long, low snout. Long thin neck. Back and tail armored with a row of conical spikes. Back sloped down to the shoulders. Single large claw on forefoot. Hindfoot with three claws. Tail ended in long whip-like tip.

DIET:
Herbivorous

Triassic
248–206 million yrs.

Jurassic
206–144 million yrs.

Cretaceous
144–65 million yrs.

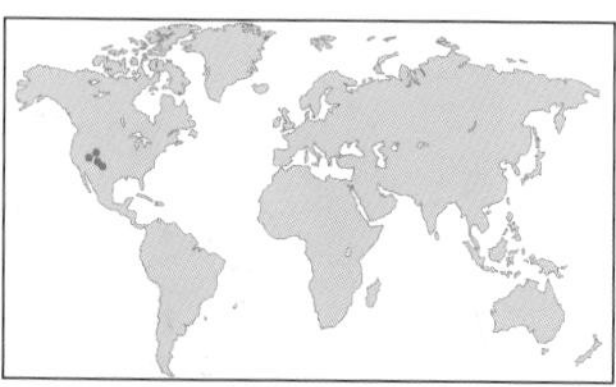

Diplodocus

(double beam)

Diplodocus owes its name to the sled-like bones under each tail vertebrae that formed a double row of "skids" along the length of the tail. Despite being one of the longest dinosaurs, it was a lightly built for a sauropod and weighed less than its shorter cousin, *Apatosaurus* (see pp.56–57). Its skull is quite modified compared to other sauropods. The teeth are restricted to the tip of the elongate muzzle, where they form a comb-like array of slender peg-shaped teeth.

The nostrils are united into a single opening on top of the head between the eyes.

Among the distinctive features of *Diplodocus* and its relatives are its particularly short forelimbs. Perhaps this was an adaptation to reducing weight at the front of the animal so that it could rear up and rest upon its tail while feeding at great heights. The "skids" below may have protected the nerves and blood-vessels of the tail from being crushed.

ID FACT FILE

LENGTH:
115 ft (35 m)

TIME:
Late Jurassic

CLASSIFICATION:
Saurischia
Sauropodomorpha
Sauropoda
Neosauropoda

DESCRIPTION:
Like Diplodocus but larger and with relatively shorter legs.

DIET:
Herbivorous

Seismosaurus

(earthquake lizard)

Looking like an oversized version of *Diplodocus* (indeed one palaeontologist has suggested that the only known specimen is merely a large *Diplodocus* (see pp. 58–59), this animal may have been the longest animal to have ever lived. However, like *Diplodocus*, it was not particularly heavily-built. The main distinguishing feature between *Seismosaurus* and other diplodocids is its relatively short legs. Indeed, it has been described as a "dinosaurian dachshund."

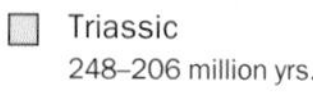
Triassic
248–206 million yrs.

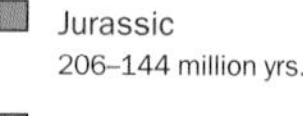
Jurassic
206–144 million yrs.

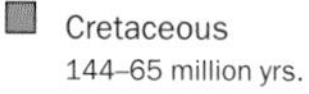
Cretaceous
144–65 million yrs.

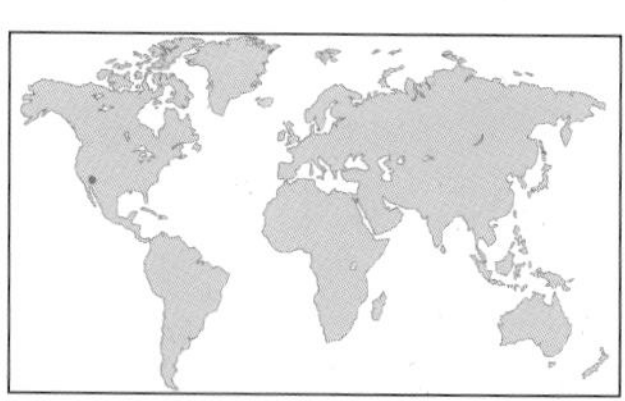

Like other diplodocids, *Seismosaurus* probably had a neck that could not be elevated from the shoulders. To browse on tree tops, the animal would have to rear up onto its back legs and tail. Some palaeontologists doubt that this was possible and suspect that the long neck improved the reach of a low browsing animal. This issue remains unresolved. It also had a long whip-like tip to its tail. It is possible, though not certain, that this could have been cracked like a whip to deter predators.

ID FACT FILE

Length:
60 ft (18 m)

Weight:
12 tons

Time:
Late Jurassic

Classification:
Saurischia
Sauropodomorpha
Sauropoda
Neosauropoda

Description:
Large,heavy-bodied quadruped with columnar limbs. Neck long but relatively shorter than in other sauropods. Head short and box-shaped. Level back. Forefoot with single large claw. Hindfoot with three claws.

Diet:
Herbivorous

Camarasaurus

(chambered lizard)

The name of this dinosaur refers to the large cavities that invade the neck and trunk vertebrae, hollowing them out so that they are a light construction of thin bony sheets. Such vertebrae are characteristic of advanced sauropods (neosauropods), and in life were probably filled with a system of air sacs that grew from outpockets of the lungs. Birds today have similar air sacs and hollowed vertebrae.

Camarasaurus was a medium-sized sauropod with a relatively short neck compared to such giants as

Triassic
248–206 million yrs.

Jurassic
206–144 million yrs.

Cretaceous
144–65 million yrs.

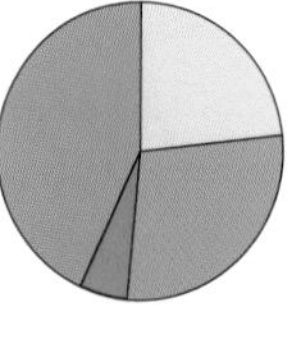

Diplodocus (see pp. 58–59) and *Brachiosaurus* (see pp. 64–65), which shared its habitat. We don't know exactly how the ecology of *Camarasaurus* differed from other sauropods, but we know from coarse scratches on its tooth enamel that it did feed on tougher vegetation than *Diplodocus* did. *Camarasaurus* had exceptionally large nasal chambers that were placed high up on its snout, which suggests that it was more related to *Brachiosaurus* than to *Diplodocus*.

Brachiosaurus

(arm lizard)

Brachiosaurus is the largest dinosaur for which we have most of the skeleton. Larger sauropods, such as *Argentinasaurus*, did exist, but these are known from just a few bones.

ID FACT FILE

LENGTH:
70 ft (21 m)

WEIGHT:
28 tons

TIME:
Late Jurassic

CLASSIFICATION:
Saurischia
Sauropodomorpha
Sauropoda
Neosauropoda

DESCRIPTION:
Very large quadruped. Head with long, broad snout. Nose forms a hump on top of the head. Very long forelegs. Back sloped down to hips. Forefoot with single, small claw. Hindfoot with three claws. Tail short relative to other sauropods.

DIET:
Herbivorous

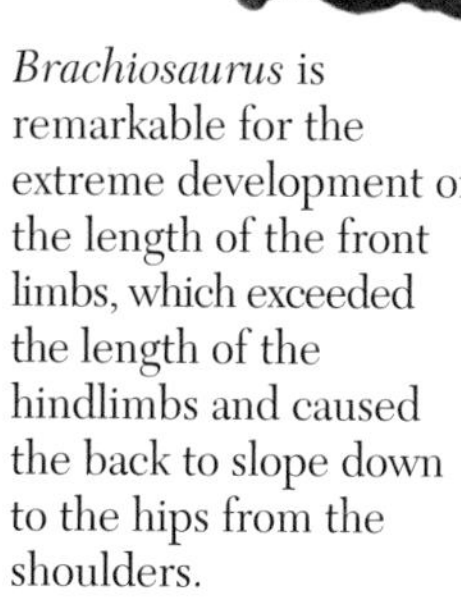

Brachiosaurus is remarkable for the extreme development of the length of the front limbs, which exceeded the length of the hindlimbs and caused the back to slope down to the hips from the shoulders.

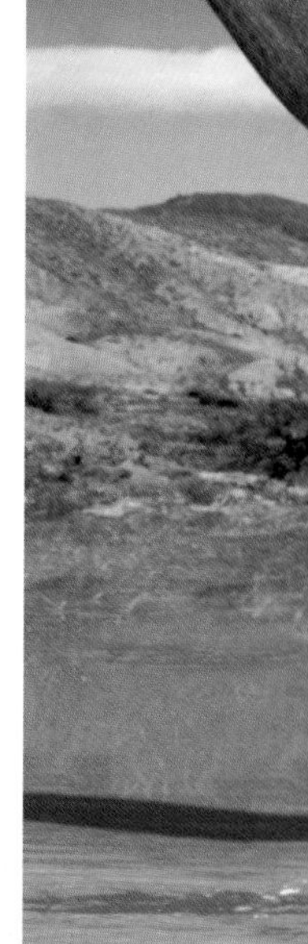

Triassic
248–206 million yrs.

Jurassic
206–144 million yrs.

Cretaceous
144–65 million yrs.

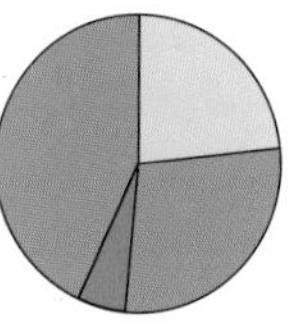

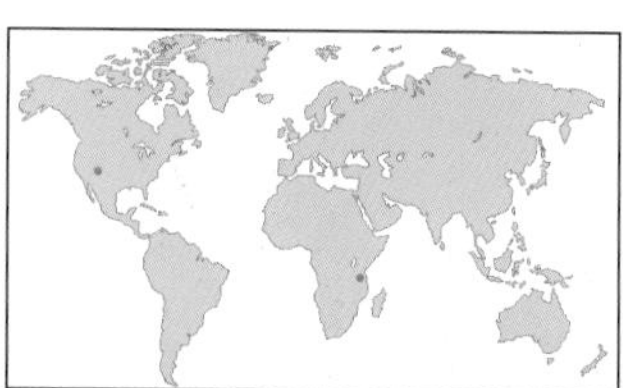

This obviously raised the base of the neck, which enabled *Brachiosaurus* to browse at higher levels than other contemporary sauropods (except perhaps diplodocids feeding in an upright stance). Despite many restorations to the contrary, the vertebrae from the base of the neck suggest that it could not raise its neck into a vertical pose. Like *Camarasaurus* (see pp. 62–63), *Brachiosaurus* had very large nasal chambers that were placed far back on its head. They formed a hump that lay behind its broad muzzle. Like *Dryosaurus* (see pp. 44–45), *Brachiosaurus* is found in both Africa and North America.

ID FACT FILE

LENGTH:
20 ft (6 m)

WEIGHT:
55lb (25 kg)

TIME:
Early Jurassic

CLASSIFICATION:
Saurischia
Theropoda
Ceratosauria

DESCRIPTION:
Medium-sized, lightly built biped. Head long with two, thin, semicircular crests on top. Neck slender. Hands with four fingers and feet with four toes. Long flexible tail.

DIET:
Carnivorous

Triassic
248–206 million yrs.

Jurassic
206–144 million yrs.

Cretaceous
144–65 million yrs.

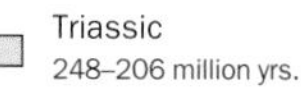

Dilophosaurus

(double-crested lizard)

Dilophosaurus is a moderately large ceratosaur that is quite closely related to the coelophysid family (see *Coelophysis* pp. 22–23). Like them, it had a four-fingered hand and a curious notch in its upper jaw. It differed from the coelophysids in being larger and more heavily built with a deeper skull.

However, the most outstanding characteristic of *Dilophosaurus* was the paired, semicircular plates that grew on top of its head.

These plates were so thin that they would not have withstood any forceful blows and therefore were almost certainly used as display structures.

The teeth of *Dilophosaurus* were unusual as well, being a lot longer and thinner than the teeth of other predatory dinosaurs. These teeth and the rather weak joint between the tip of the snout and the upper jaws suggest that it did not tackle very large struggling prey. It may have specialized on smaller game such as little reptiles, amphibians, and fish.

ID FACT FILE

LENGTH:
20 ft (6 m)

WEIGHT:
990 lb (450 kg)

TIME:
Late Jurassic

CLASSIFICATION:
Saurischia
Theropoda
Ceratosauria

DESCRIPTION:
Medium-sized, heavily built biped. Neck short and head large and deep. Paired horns in front of each eye and a single horn on top of the snout. Arms short, hands with four fingers. Feet with three large toes and a reduced third toe. Long, deep, flexible tail.

DIET:
Carnivorous

Ceratosaurus

(horned lizard)

The short powerful neck and large head of *Ceratosaurus* gave it the appearance of a carnosaur. Nevertheless, many features of its skeleton show that it was a more primitive kind of theropod and that its real relationships lie with the early *Coelophysis* (see pp. 22–23) and *Dilophosaurus* (see pp. 66–67).

These features include a four-fingered hand and fusion of the different bones of the hip. *Ceratosaurus* had a distinctive appearance,

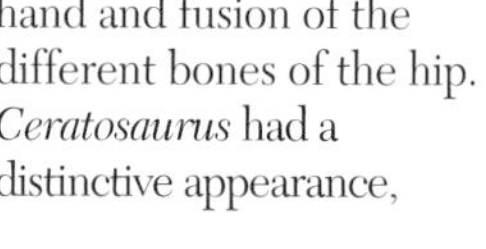

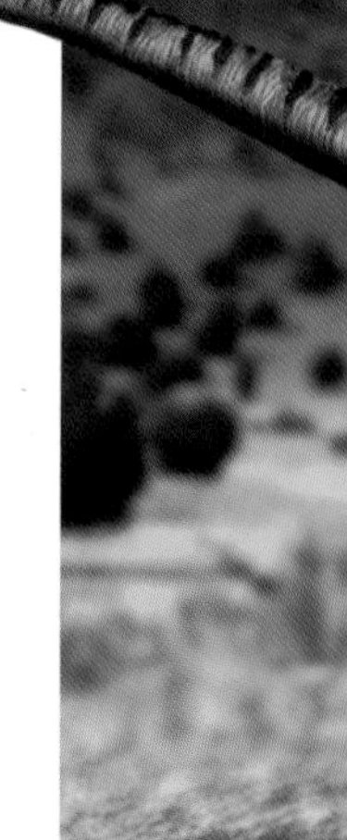

Triassic
248–206 million yrs.

Jurassic
206–144 million yrs.

Cretaceous
144–65 million yrs.

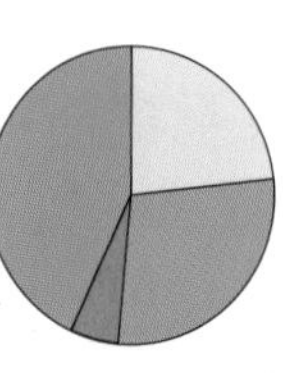

with two short horns in front of each eye and a taller flattened horn on top of the snout, just behind its nostrils. It is also the only theropod known to have had a row of bony armor studs extending along its back.

Ceratosaurus also had a deep muscular tail that would have been supple all the way to its tip, another feature that sets it apart from the carnosaurs which were tetanuran ("stiff tailed") theropods.

ID FACT FILE

LENGTH:
20 ft (6 m)

WEIGHT:
440 lb (200 kg)

TIME:
Late Jurassic

CLASSIFICATION:
Saurischia
Theropoda
Ceratosauria

DESCRIPTION:
Medium-sized, lightly built, long-bodied biped. Long, thin neck. Slender weak arms with long thin fingers. Long legs with three-toed feet.

DIET:
Probably carnivorous.

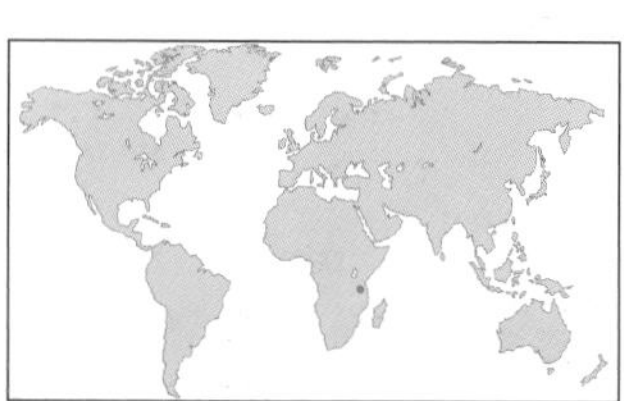

Triassic
248–206 million yrs.

Jurassic
206–144 million yrs.

Cretaceous
144–65 million yrs.

Elaphrosaurus

(light-weight lizard)

It is unfortunate that the only known skeleton of *Elaphrosaurus* is missing the skull. This plus the unusual features of its skeleton make it a difficult theropod to classify. It was once classified as a coelurosaur based upon its slender build. It has even been called a primitive ancestor of the Cretaceous "ostrich mimic" dinosaurs, such as *Struthiomimus* (see pp. 202–203). We now think that it is a ceratosaur like *Coelophysis* (see pp. 22–23).

Among ceratosaurs, its straight upper arm bone with reduced muscle attachments resembled the upper arm bone of the abelisaurid *Carnotaurus* (see pp. 180–181).

It is quite probable that *Elaphrosaurus* was an early relative of the abelisaurids. Although abelisaurids and their relatives are widespread and diverse in the Cretaceous of the Southern Hemisphere, no others are known from the Jurassic. Although no skull has been found, it is most likely that, like all other ceratosaurs, *Elaphrosaurus* was a carnivore.

ID FACT FILE

LENGTH:
15 ft (4.5 m)

WEIGHT:
550 lb (250 kg)

TIME:
Middle Jurassic

CLASSIFICATION:
Saurischia
Theropoda
Tetanurae

DESCRIPTION:
Medium-sized biped. Head large and deep. Neck short. Arms short. Thumb with large claw. Feet with three toes. The first toe is very reduced.

DIET:
Carnivorous

Eustreptospondylus

(well-twisted spine)

The upper and lower halves of the vertebrae of the only known skeleton of *Eustreptospondylus* have not fused together, suggesting that the individual was not fully-grown at the time death. It is not known how much bigger it could have got. It appears to have been a typical early tetanuran theropod with a large deep skull, curved blade-like teeth and short arms. A number of features, such as the lack of little horns

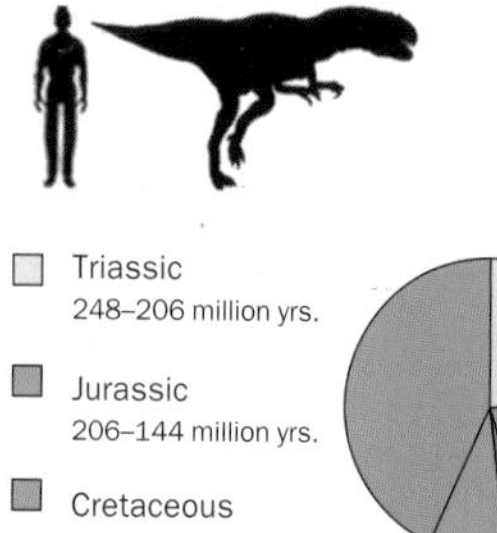

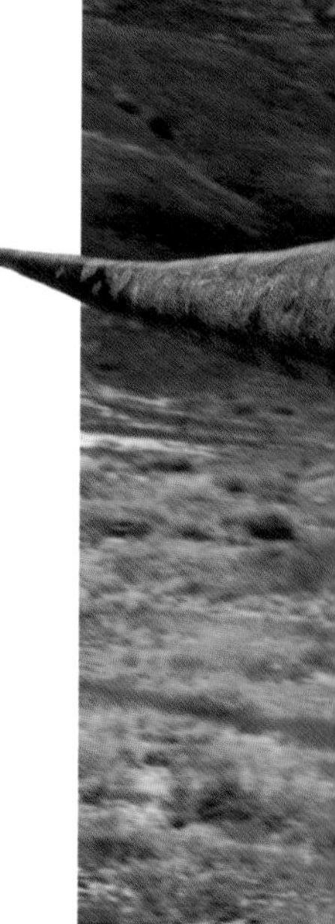

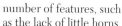

Triassic
248–206 million yrs.

Jurassic
206–144 million yrs.

Cretaceous
144–65 million yrs.

in front of the eyes and broad pubic bones, suggest that it was a close relative of a particularly large and fearsome theropod from North America called *Torvosaurus*. *Eustreptospondylus* and *Torvosaurus* also share a large thumb claw and a short forearm with the bizarre spinosaurids (see *Baryonyx*, pp. 184–185), suggesting that the two groups might be related.

Eustreptospondylus probably lived on the small islands that dotted the sea in which it was buried. It may have been an island hopping beachcomber.

ID FACT FILE

Length:
23 ft (7 m)

Time:
Middle Jurassic

Classification:
Saurischia
Theropoda
Tetanurae

Description:
Large, heavily-built biped. Head large with many sharp blade-like teeth in the jaws. Arms short but powerful. Feet with three weight supporting toes and a reduced first toe.

Diet:
Carnivorous, other dinosaurs.

Megalosaurus

(big lizard)

Megalosaurus was the first dinosaur to receive a scientific name. It was named by William Buckland in 1824, and was based on a piece of jaw with large blade-like teeth from Stonesfield, England. Since it was the first to be named, many subsequent discoveries of carnivorous dinosaurs from all around the world were attributed to this genus. However, we know that nearly all of these identifications are wrong and that only material from Stonesfield can be properly called *Megalosaurus*.

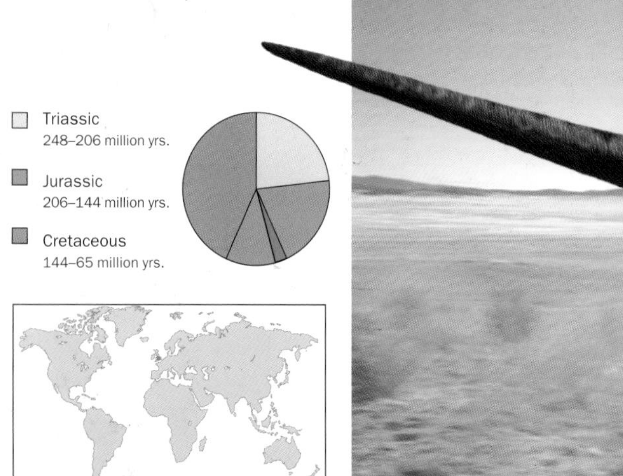

Despite having such a long history, we still know little about this dinosaur. It was a large carnivorous theropod that would have looked superficially like a carnosaur such as *Allosaurus* (see pp. 80–81).

However, it had certain primitive characteristics of the hip and thigh that indicate that, although it was a tetanuran (stiff-tailed theropods that are more closely related to birds than to ceratosaurs), it was neither a carnosaur, nor a coelurosaur. It might have been a relative of *Eusteptospondylus* (see pp. 72–73).

ID FACT FILE

LENGTH:
16½ ft (5 m)

TIME:
Middle Jurassic

CLASSIFICATION:
Saurischia
Theropoda
Tetanurae
Carnosauria

DESCRIPTION:
Medium-sized biped. Head long and low (for a carnosaur). Tall crest from above the eyes to the snout tip. Neck short. Arms short.

DIET:
Carnivorous, other dinosaurs.

Monolophosaurus

(single crested lizard)

Monolophosaurus is known from a beautiful skull and partial skeleton found in the Gurbantunggut Desert of China. It was a small carnosaur, possibly belonging to the allosaurid family. Its most distinctive feature was a tall crest running along the top of its skull. CAT scans indicate that this crest was a delicate hollow structure. It was probably used for display.

Carnosaurs are characterized by large deep and narrow heads filled with blade-like teeth, mounted short

Triassic
248–206 million yrs.

Jurassic
206–144 million yrs.

Cretaceous
144–65 million yrs.

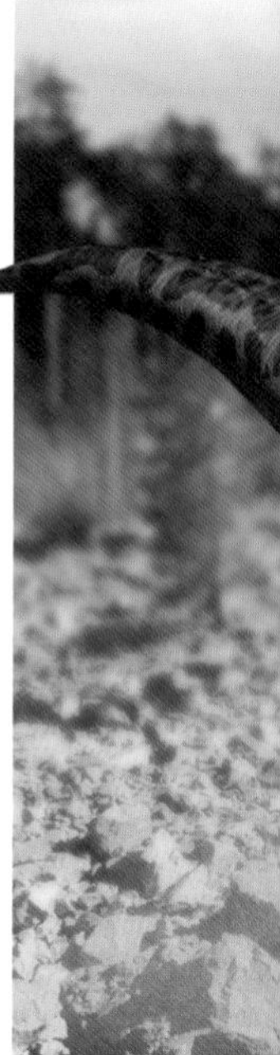

necks, and short but powerful arms. They were predators that may have killed their prey by delivering several quick slashing bites.

Despite their fearsome nature, carnosaurs have certain bird-like features, including a three fingered hand, a braced joint between the upper ankle bone and the main lower leg bone, and a tail that was stiff and inflexible at its tip. These features indicate that carnosaurs were more closely related to birds than they were to ceratosaurian theropods.

ID FACT FILE

LENGTH:
26 ft (8 m)

TIME:
Early Jurassic

CLASSIFICATION:
Saurischia
Theropoda
Tetanurae
Carnosauria

DESCRIPTION:
Large biped. Large, deep head. Tall, forward curving, plate-like crest in front of eyes.

DIET:
Carnivorous, prosauropods.

Cryolophosaurus

(frozen-crested lizard)

This is currently the only named dinosaur known from Antarctica. It was found on Mount Kirkpatrick, close to the South Pole. Nevertheless, Antarctica had a more northerly position in the Early Jurassic and the global climate was warmer. Therefore, it is unlikely that *Cryolophosaurus* ever had to contend with freezing conditions.

Cryolophosaurus had a large, deep skull, rather like that of *Allosaurus* (see pp. 80–81) but

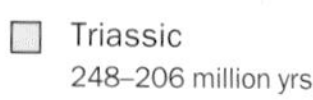

Triassic
248–206 million yrs.

Jurassic
206–144 million yrs.

Cretaceous
144–65 million yrs.

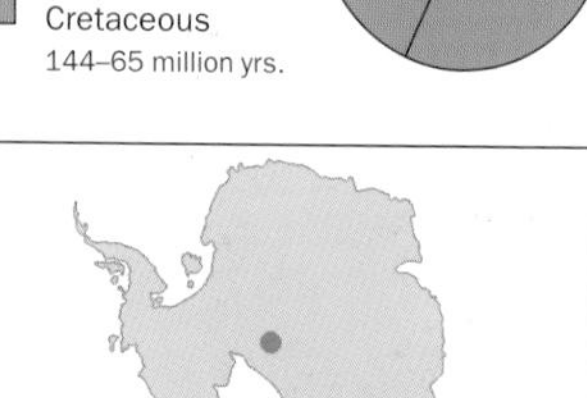

with a most unusual crest.
This crest was a thin, ridged plate that was placed on top of the head, just in front of the eyes. This plate, which curved forward, was unlike most dinosaur crests in that it was flattened front-to-back and was broad from sided to side.

Apart from this unusual feature, *Cryolophosaurus* was a fairly primitive carnosaur, which keeps it the earliest known member of the group. Fragmentary remains of prosauropods were found with it, which it almost certainly preyed upon.

ID FACT FILE

LENGTH:
26 ft (8 m)

WEIGHT:
1 ton

TIME:
Late Jurassic

CLASSIFICATION:
Saurischia
Theropoda
Tetanurae
Carnosauria

DESCRIPTION:
Large, heavily-built biped. Large, deep head with small horns in front of each eye. Short, thick neck. Short, powerful arms. Three fingers with large curved claws.

DIET:
Carnivorous

Allosaurus

(other lizard)

Allosaurus is the most common large predator of the Late Jurassic. Most remains are from Western North America, but some have also been found in Portugal. It was a fairly typical carnosaur in outward appearance.

It had a large, deep head on a short powerful neck and short, strong arms tipped with three large claws. Its long

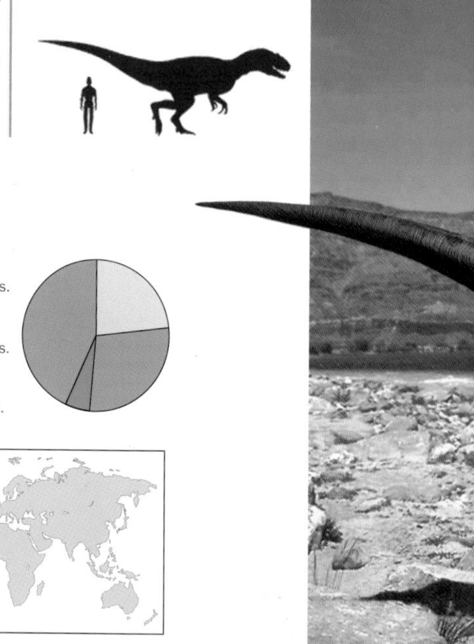

Triassic
248–206 million yrs.

Jurassic
206–144 million yrs.

Cretaceous
144–65 million yrs.

legs were robust and did not have the speedy running proportions of coelurosaurs. The last third of the tail was thin and stiff, as is typical of most tetanurans.

Studies of its jaw and skull mechanics indicate that the animal used its upper jaws like a hatchet when attacking its prey. Support for this idea comes from the extremely wide gape that the jaw joint allowed and the shock-absorbing ability of its skull. Its skull was decorated for display with little horns in front of each eye and a ridge on each side of the snout.

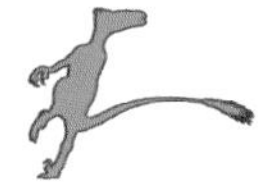

ID FACT FILE

Length:
3 ft (1 m)

Weight:
8 lb (3.5 kg)

Time:
Late Jurassic

Classification:
Saurischia
Theropoda
Tetanurae
Coelurosauria

Description:
Small, lightly built biped. Moderately small head with a pointed snout. Neck long. Arms short. Probably three small fingers. Legs long with three large toes and a reduced first toe. Tail very long with a stiff tip. Covered with "protofeathers."

Diet:
Carnivorous, small mammals, lizards

Compsognathus

(pretty jaw)

For more than a century *Compsognathus* held the title of the smallest known adult dinosaur. With the inclusion of birds in the Dinosauria, this honor now belongs to the bee hummingbird which is 2½ in (6.2 cm) long. If we exclude birds from consideration, the newly discovered *Microraptor* (see pp. 220–221) is now the smallest. *Compsognathus* was an inhabitant of the small desert islands that were also home to *Archaeopteryx* (see pp. 86–87).

Triassic
248–206 million yrs.

Jurassic
206–144 million yrs.

Cretaceous
144–65 million yrs.

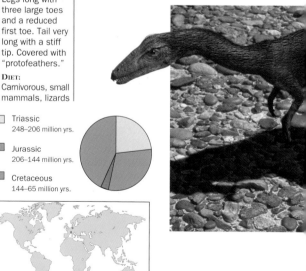

The skeleton of a lizard has been found in the ribcage of one of the two known *Compsognathus* skeletons. A closely related genus from China, *Sinosauropteryx* has been found with a small mammal in its abdominal cavity. These specimens amply demonstrate that compsognathids were voracious predators of small terrestrial vertebrates.

Sinosauropteryx also had a coat of unbranched, hair-like "protofeathers" preserved around it, which was probably present on *Compsognathus* as well. The protofeathers could well have acted as insulation, suggesting that compsognathids—and other coelurosaurs with protofeathers—may have developed "warm-bloodedness."

ID FACT FILE

LENGTH:
6½ ft (2 m)

WEIGHT:
30 lb (13 kg)

TIME:
Late Jurassic

CLASSIFICATION:
Saurischia
Theropoda
Tetanurae
Coelurosauria

DESCRIPTION:
Small, lightly built biped. Small head with large teeth and a blunt snout. Neck long. Moderately long arms. Slender hind legs. Three large toes. First toe very small. Long tail with stiff tip.

DIET:
Carnivorous, small mammals, lizards

Triassic
248–206 million yrs.

Jurassic
206–144 million yrs.

Cretaceous
144–65 million yrs.

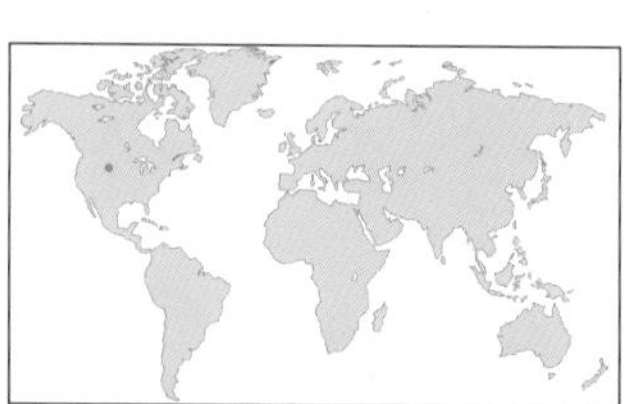

Ornitholestes

(bird thief)

Ornitholestes was a typical small coelurosaur. Coelurosaurs were a group of tetanuran theropods that underwent a spectacular evolutionary radiation in the Late Jurassic to produce such different groups as tyrannosaurids, therizinosaurids, ornithomimids, oviraptorids, dromaeosaurids, and even birds.

Among other features in common, all these dinosaurs have air-filled cavities invading various bones at the back of the

skull and a broad depression surrounding the hole in the skull in front of the eye. *Ornitholestes* is close to what palaeontologists think the ancestor of these groups would have looked like. It was small and lightly built with a long neck and long grasping hands with curved claws.

Many recent reconstructions of *Ornithlestes* give it a flattened horn on its nose. Recent cleaning of the specimen has shown that this is in error and that the appearance of the base of a nose horn was caused by damage to the snout.

ID FACT FILE

LENGTH:
18 in (45 cm)

WEIGHT:
11 oz (300 g)

TIME:
Late Jurassic

CLASSIFICATION:
Saurischia
Theropoda
Tetanurae, Aves
Coelurosauria

DESCRIPTION:
Small biped. Triangular head with pointed snout. Very long arms feathered to form broad wings. Three-clawed fingers; three large toes. Short, stiff, feathered tail.

DIET:
Carnivorous, small animals.

Archaeopteryx

(ancient feather)

This is perhaps the most famous vertebrate fossil of all because it provided early evidence of animal intermediate in structure between two classes of animals, supporting Darwin's theory of evolution

The stunningly preserved fossils showed *Archaeopteryx* had a coat of feathers and a "wishbone," or furcula, in its shoulder girdle. Among modern animals these features can only be found in birds.

Triassic
248–206 million yrs.

Jurassic
206–144 million yrs.

Cretaceous
144–65 million yrs.

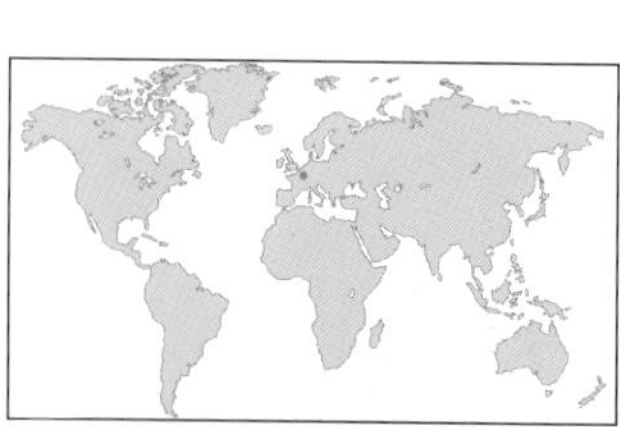

However, *Archaeopteryx* displayed such reptilian features as teeth and a long bony tail, which no modern bird has. It soon became clear that among reptiles, *Archaeopteryx* most closely resembled theropod dinosaurs. Indeed it is almost a bone for bone match with the dromaeosaurids (see pp. 218–225), the closest relatives of the birds. *Archaeopteryx* lived on small arid islands in a lagoon where it may have spent its time clambering about in low shrubs. It had small conical teeth ideal for capturing insects and other small prey.

Hybodus

(blunt cone-tooth)

Hybodus was perhaps the most abundant shark during the Mesozoic Era. It differed from modern sharks in having jaws that did not protrude when biting. It also lacked the pointed overhanging snout that is typical of modern sharks. Like all sharks, its skeleton was made of cartilage, which quickly decays after death. As a consequence most *Hybodus* fossils are isolated teeth.

ID FACT FILE

LENGTH:
8 ft (2.5 m)

TIME:
Middle Triassic to Late Cretaceous

CLASSIFICATION:
Vertebrata Chondrichthyes

DESCRIPTION:
Medium-sized, to large, shark. Jaws not set back from snout tip. Two dorsal fins each with a sharp spine. A pair of small hooked spines behind each eye.

DIET:
Carnivorous, fish, squid-like molluscs, small marine reptiles.

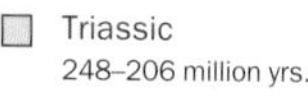

Triassic
248–206 million yrs.

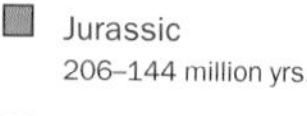

Jurassic
206–144 million yrs.

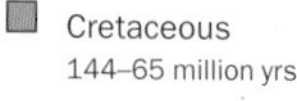

Cretaceous
144–65 million yrs.

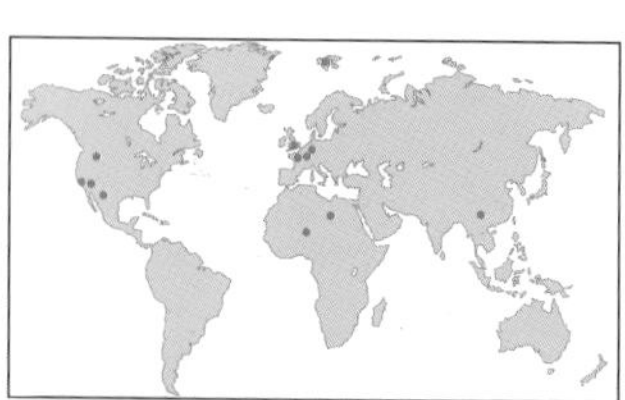

Fortunately, the exceptional Early Jurassic locality of Holzmaden, Germany, has preserved a number of complete skeletons. From these we know that it had two dorsal fins, each with a sharp spine in front of it. There were also small hook-shaped spines above and behind each eye.

The tall pointed teeth show that *Hybodus* was adapted to catching and tearing fast-moving and slippery prey. In this respect, *Hybodus* differs from its close relatives, which had flat crushing teeth adapted for dealing with shell-fish.

ID FACT FILE

LENGTH:
8 ft (2.5 m)

TIME:
Early Jurassic

CLASSIFICATION:
Reptilia
Diapsida
Ichthyosauria

DESCRIPTION:
Torpedo-shaped body. Snout long and thin with many pointed teeth. Triangular, paddle-like limbs. Front limbs much larger than hind limbs. Triangular dorsal fin. Crescent-shaped tail fin.

DIET:
Carnivorous, Fish, and squid-like molluscs.

Triassic
248–206 million yrs.

Jurassic
206–144 million yrs.

Cretaceous
144–65 million yrs.

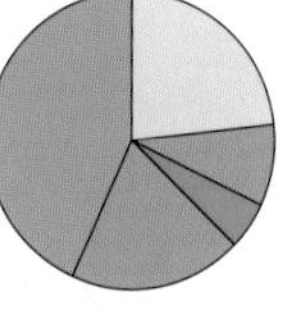

Stenopterygius

(narrow fin)

Stenopterygius was a common member of the most highly adapted group of marine reptiles, the icthyosaurs. Their name means "fish lizard" and indeed they looked more like fish than reptiles. Nevertheless, they lacked gills and had many reptilian skeletal traits. Very fine specimens of *Stenopterygius* from Holzmaden, Germany preserve an outline of the soft tissues and show that they had a shark-like dorsal fin and a crescent-shaped tail fin. The spinal column has a distinct bend at the tail base with the column continuing down into the lower lobe of the tail. The upper lobe was unsupported by bone. Other *Stenopterygius* skeletons show numerous embryonic skeletons inside, some preserved half way out of their mother's birth canal! This is proof that ichthyosaurs spent their entire lives at sea and did not return to land to lay eggs. Its snout formed a long beak lined with sharp teeth. It was clearly a fast swimming hunter.

ID FACT FILE

LENGTH:
11½ ft (3.5 m)

TIME:
Late Jurassic

CLASSIFICATION:
Reptilia
Diapsida
Ichthyosauria

DESCRIPTION:
Short, thick-bodied ichthyosaur. Head with long, thin snout and enormous eyes. Short broad paddle-like limbs. Narrow tail base with deep crescent-shaped tail fin.

DIET:
Carnivorous, Fish, and squid-like molluscs.

Opthalmosaurus

(eye lizard)

Opthalmosaurus lived after *Stenopterygius* (see pp. 90–91). It differed from that ichthyosaur in having broader paddles; a more compact body; and a sharper kink in its tail, suggesting that the tail fin was shorter and deeper—like that of a swordfish. All these features indicate that *Opthalmosaurus* was a very fast swimmer.

Another peculiar feature of *Opthalmosaurus* was its enormous eyes.

Triassic
248–206 million yrs.

Jurassic
206–144 million yrs.

Cretaceous
144–65 million yrs.

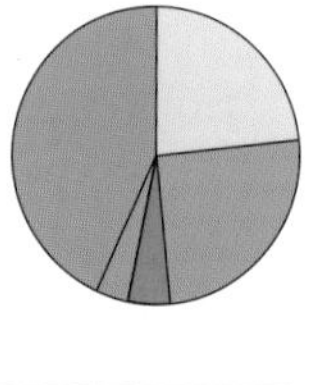

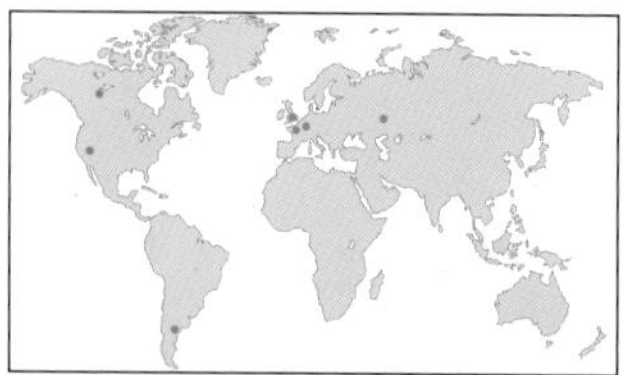

The size of ichthyosaur eye can be estimated accurately because they were reinforced with large bony plates, which formed a ring around the iris.

An *Opthalmosaurus* eyeball was almost 10 in (25 cm) across, making it one of the largest in the animal kingdom relative to body size. This big eye suggests that it could see in low light conditions, so perhaps it was diving to great depths. Further evidence for deep diving comes from their bone microtexture, which shows frequent damage caused by decompression sickness, or the "bends."

ID FACT FILE

LENGTH:
10 ft (3 m)

TIME:
Early Jurassic

CLASSIFICATION:
Reptilia, Diapsida Sauropterygia Plesiosauria

DESCRIPTION:
Head small and short with long, pointed teeth. Neck several times longer than the skull. Body short and wide. Limbs form elongate paddles. Tail short.

DIET:
Carnivorous, fish, and squid-like molluscs.

Plesiosaurus

(nearly a lizard)

Plesiosaurians were a successful group of aquatic reptiles during the Jurassic and Cretaceous. There were two basic types, the long-necked, small-headed plesiosaurs and the short-necked, large-headed pliosaurs.

Plesiosaurus was an early example of the former group. It had a flexible neck that was about as long as its body. Plesiosaurs had long, sharp teeth for catching slippery prey such as fish or squid-like animals.

There has been controversy about how plesiosaurs may

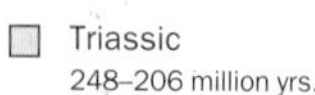

Triassic
248–206 million yrs.

Jurassic
206–144 million yrs.

Cretaceous
144–65 million yrs.

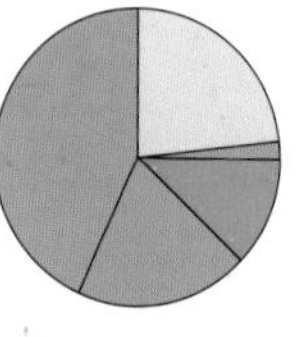

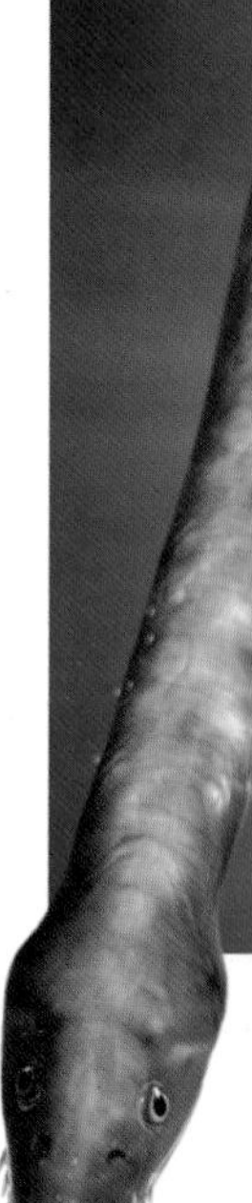

have swum. Underwater rowing is not feasible without paddles that can be folded up, and underwater flying seems to be ruled out by the structure of the hip and shoulder girdles, which do not allow the paddles to be lifted above horizontally. The best solution seems to be that they swam like modern sea lions, which use a combination of rowing and flying-like motions of their paddles to power them through the water.

ID FACT FILE

LENGTH:
20 ft (6 m)

TIME:
Early Jurassic

CLASSIFICATION:
Reptilia, Diapsida
Sauropterygia
Plesiosauria

DESCRIPTION:
Long, broad head with large teeth. Neck slightly longer than the skull. Body short and wide. Limbs form elongated paddles. Tail short.

DIET:
Fish, other marine reptiles.

Rhomaelosaurus

(robust lizard)

Rhomaelosaurus was an early pliosaur, the big-headed plesiosaurians that specialized on larger prey than their long-necked ancestors. It displays some signs of its ancestry as its neck is relatively longer than in later pliosaurs; it is slightly longer than the length of the skull. In all species, however, the head is broad, flat, and relatively larger than in plesiosaurs. The ends of the jaws

Triassic
248–206 million yrs.

Jurassic
206–144 million yrs.

Cretaceous
144–65 million yrs.

bear a rounded expansion. This expanded tip was armed with a rosette of enlarged, interlocking teeth much like those of modern crocodiles. *Rhomaelosaurus* probably used them in a similar manner, holding tightly onto its prey while the animal rolled in the water, thus tearing off a large chunk of flesh. Its prey would have included large fish and other marine reptiles.

ID FACT FILE

LENGTH:
10 ft (3 m)

TIME:
Middle to Late Jurassic

CLASSIFICATION:
Reptilia, Diapsida
Archosauria
Crurotarsi
Crocodyliformes

DESCRIPTION:
Long, thin snouted crocodile. Skin smooth. Limbs form small paddles.Half-moon shaped tail fin.

DIET:
Carnivorous, fish.

Metriorhynchus

(middle [-sized] beak)

Metriorhynchus was a sea-going relative of modern crocodiles. It was very well adapted to its marine existence and probably only ventured onto land to lay its eggs. Although found mainly in Europe, relatives of *Metriorhynchus* spread throughout the warm tropical seas of the world.

Its limbs had become modified into paddles, and it had lost the bony armor

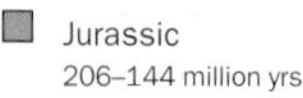

Triassic
248–206 million yrs.

Jurassic
206–144 million yrs.

Cretaceous
144–65 million yrs.

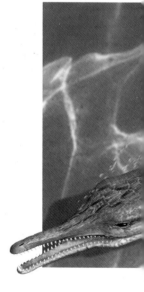

plates that all other crurotarsans have (see *Postosuchus*, pp. 26–27), and it had developed a fish-like tail. We can tell that the tail was modified in this manner because, like ichthyosaurs, the tail contains a strong downward bend.

Its long, narrow snout and sharp conical teeth are typical of fish hunting animals and this is, without doubt, what it fed upon. The narrow jaws reduced water resistance and allowed them to be closed quickly underwater. The diapsid skull openings had become very large in this animal, suggesting that its jaw muscles were very long and that its gape was wide.

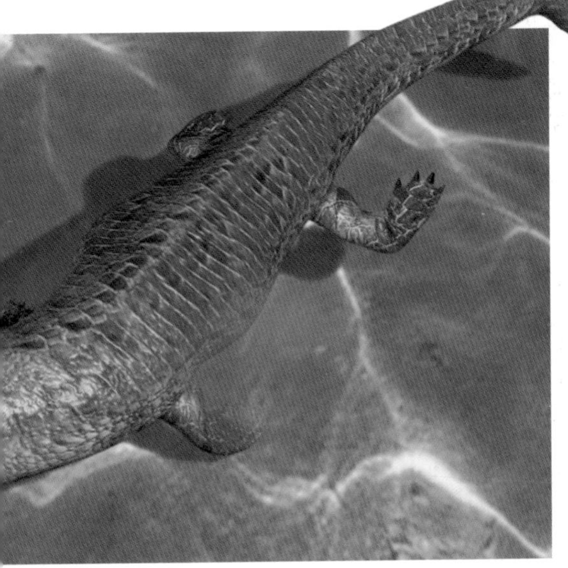

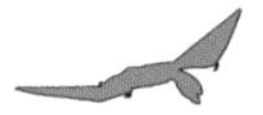

ID FACT FILE

LENGTH:
Wingspan 24 in (60 cm)

TIME:
Late Jurassic

CLASSIFICATION:
Reptilia, Diapsida Archosauria Ornithodira Pterosauria Rhamphorhynchoidea

DESCRIPTION:
Small flying reptile. Long arms with three free fingers, long fourth finger supporting wing membrane; second membrane between legs. Tail long with thickened tip.

DIET:
Carnivorous, insects.

Sordes

(devil)

Sordes was a tiny pterosaur (flying reptile) related to *Rhamphorynchus* (see pp. 102–103). The spectacular preservation of its remains (which are found in shales that were laid down in an ancient lake) has helped clear up many aspects of pterosaur anatomy.

These fossils show that *Sordes* had a pelt of hair-like filaments. This would have insulated the animal, indicating that the animal was endothermic ("warm-blooded").

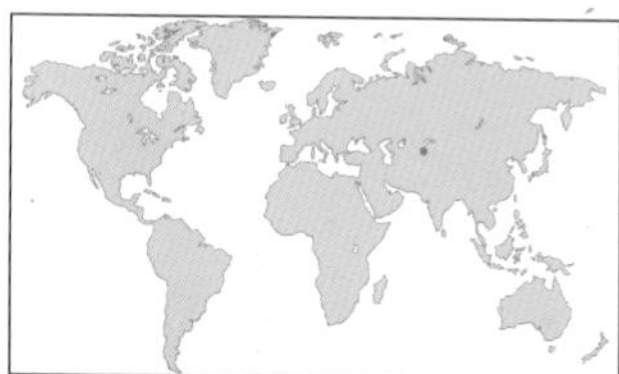

Since flying is such an energy demanding activity, it is likely that all pterosaurs were hairy and endothermic. The fossils also show that the wing membrane stretched from the tip of the elongated fourth finger to the ankle. A second membrane spanned the space between its hind legs and it was held tight by the spine-like fifth toe of each foot. These membranes were supported by stiff fibers that ran from the arms and legs to the trailing edge of the membranes.

It differed from *Rhamphorhynchus* in having vertically oriented teeth (for catching insect prey) and by lacking an expanded tail-vane.

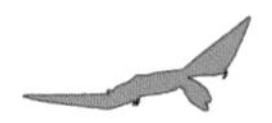

Rhamphorhynchus

(beaked snout)

ID FACT FILE

WINGSPAN:
6 ft (1.75 m)

TIME:
Late Jurassic

CLASSIFICATION:
Reptilia, Diapsida
Archosauria
Ornithodira
Pterosauria
Rhamphorhynch-oidea

DESCRIPTION:
Small flying reptile. Like Sordes but with sharp, pointed snout tip and a diamond-shaped tail-vane.

DIET:
Carnivorous, fish.

Rhamphorhynchus was without doubt a fishing pterosaur. Its jaws bore a pointed beak at their tips and were filled with long, forward pointing, spiky teeth that produced a structure excellent for spearing and holding slippery prey.

The downward bend of its lower jaw suggests that it may have skimmed surface waters while flying, as some seabirds do.

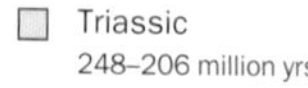

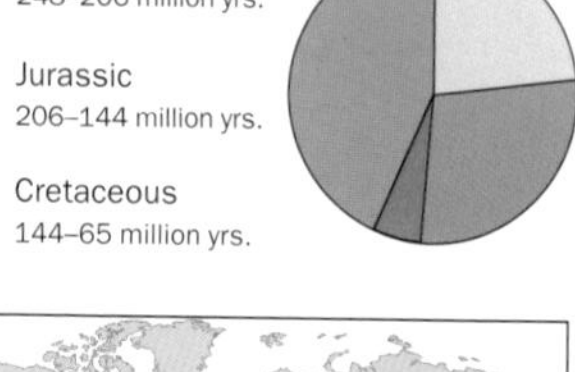

Most remains of this pterosaur come from the famous Solnhoffen Limestone, a lagoonal deposit that also preserved *Archaeopteryx* (see pp. 86–87), as well as other well known extinct creatures. The fine preservation of this deposit has produced a number of specimens with impressions of the wing membrane.

These show that the wing was narrow for most of its length and that many rod-like fibers stiffened it. The tail also had a diamond-shaped vane at its tip, which was probably used as a rudder during flight.

ID FACT FILE

WINGSPAN:
20 in (50 cm)

TIME:
Late Jurassic

CLASSIFICATION:
Reptilia, Diapsida
Archosauria
Ornithodira
Pterosauria
Rhamphorhynch-oidea

DESCRIPTION:
Small flying reptile. Head short, deep and broad. Arms long. Three free fingers. Fourth finger very long supporting wing membrane. Second membrane stretched between the legs. Four toes with claws, fifth toe spine-like. Tail shorter than body.

DIET:
Carnivorous, insects.

Triassic
248–206 million yrs.

Jurassic
206–144 million yrs.

Cretaceous
144–65 million yrs.

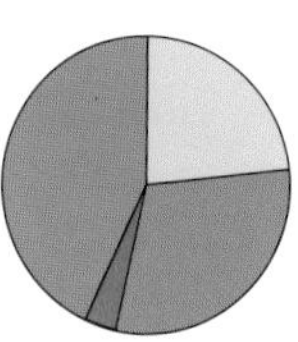

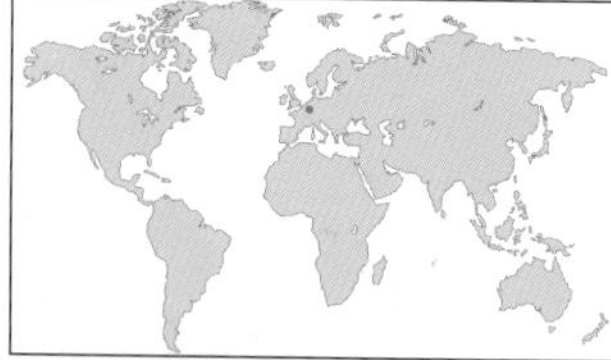

Anurognathus

(tail-less jaw)

The unusual name of this pterosaur refers to the resemblance of its jaws to the jaws of a frog (called anurans by scientists).

Unlike most other pterosaurs, *Anurognathus* had a short, broad snout that would not had been useful for catching aquatic animals but would have been good for catching flying insects.

Thus, *Anurognathus* may have lived further inland than other pterosaurs. This would explain why only one skeleton has ever been found, since the lagoonal deposits in which it was found have produced dozens of *Pterodactylus* and *Rhamphorhynchus* skeletons. *Anurognathus* had a very short tail-like pterodactyloid pterosaurs, but also had a long spine-like fifth toe and short neck vertebrae characteristic of rhamphornychoids. For these reasons *Anurognathus* is classified as a ramphorhynchoid that evolved a short tail at the same time as pterodactyloids.

ID FACT FILE

WINGSPAN:
8 ft (2.5 m)

TIME:
Late Jurassic

CLASSIFICATION:
Reptilia, Diapsida
Archosauria
Ornithodira
Pterosauria
Pterodactyloidea

DESCRIPTION:
Small flying reptile. Head with long narrow jaws. Neck long. Arms long. Three free fingers. Fourth finger very long supporting wing membrane. Second membrane stretched between the legs. Four webbed toes. Tail reduced to stump.

DIET:
Carnivorous, small invertebrates.

Pterodactlyus

(wing finger)

Petrodactylus was an early member of the pterodactyloid group of pterosaurs which completely supplanted the rhamphorhynchoids in the Cretaceous.

Pterodactyloids differ from rhamphorhynchoids in having a reduced stump for a tail and in having only four toes (the spine-like fifth toe is missing). *Pterodactylus* had a rather simple cranial design without any of the extravagant crests of other pterodactyloids.

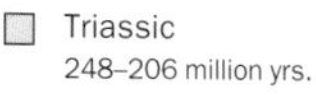

Triassic
248–206 million yrs.

Jurassic
206–144 million yrs.

Cretaceous
144–65 million yrs.

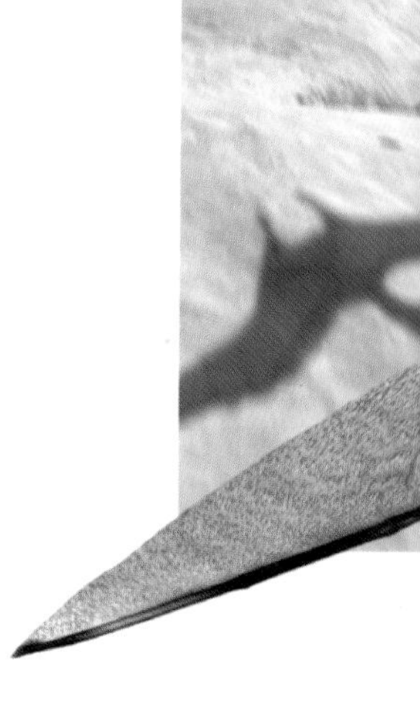

Soft tissue impressions show that it had broad wings that attached to the knee and webbed feet. It had a long neck and a long, narrow snout with small, conical teeth placed at its tip.

The jaws resembled a pair of forceps, and it has been suggested that they were used as such to pull worms and other soft bodied invertebrates from the mud of tidal flats. This is certainly plausible, and its webbed hindfeet are also consistent with a shorebird-like lifestyle.

ID FACT FILE

Length:
4 in (10 cm)

Time:
Early Jurassic

Classification:
Synapsida
Therapsida
Mammaliaformes

Description:
Tiny sprawling quadruped. Similar to a modern shrew. Probably hairy. Ears probably simple holes. Fingers and Toes five. Moderately long thin tail.

Diet:
Carnivorous, insects and other small invertebrates.

Triassic
248–206 million yrs.

Jurassic
206–144 million yrs.

Cretaceous
144–65 million yrs.

Morganucodon

(Morgan's tooth)

Morganucodon is often portrayed as one of the earliest known mammals; however, this is not strictly true in modern classifications. It was undoubtedly a close relative of modern mammals, and would have looked a lot like a shrew. Nevertheless, it retained accessory lower jaw-bones besides the main tooth-bearing bone.

In all modern mammals, these jaw bones are transferred to the middle

ear. For this reason *Morganucodon* is classified as a mammaliaform (the larger group that includes mammals and their close relatives) but not a true mammal.

Given its small size and apparently warm-blooded metabolism, it almost certainly had a pelt of fur for insulation. It had sharp, pointed teeth that were differentiated into incisors, canines, and molars for processing its invertebrate prey.

Its remains have been found in the sediment filling ancient cave systems of South-west Britain, much like those of *Thecodontosaurus* (see pp. 12–13).

ID FACT FILE

LENGTH:
6½ ft (2 m)

TIME:
Early Cretaceous

CLASSIFICATION:
Ornithischia
Thyreophora
Ankylosauria

DESCRIPTION:
Small, heavy bodied quadruped. Head short and broad with a deep, narrow snout. Multiple rows of small keeled plates over the back. A pair of large plates on the neck and another over the shoulders. Tear-drop shaped spikes on each side of the hips.

DIET:
Herbivorous.

Minmi

(from Minmi [Crossing])

Minmi was an unusually small ankylosaur from Australia. Ankylosaurs are heavily armored relatives of the stegosaurs (see pp. 34–41). It does not fit readily into any of the main ankylosaurid families, and probably represents a unique Australian group.

The spinal column contained unique bones that laid on both sides of each vertebra. These were originally thought to be bases for muscles that could move

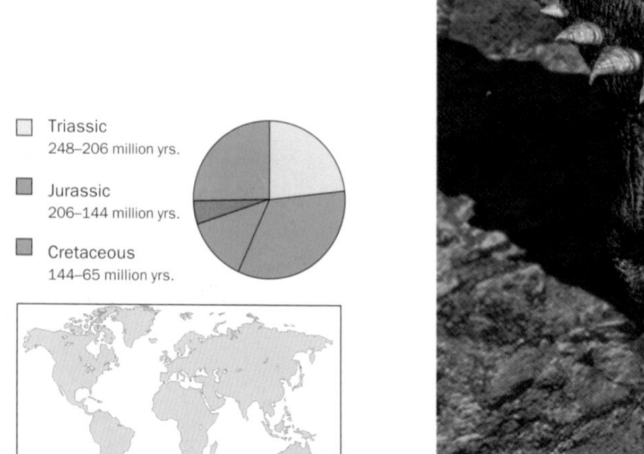

the dorsal armor plates. We now know that the dorsal armor was not especially large or elaborate and that these odd bones were more likely to be ossified tendons. The skull of *Minmi* was shaped like a pentagonal box with a very narrow snout projecting from its front. Like polacanthids and ankylosaurids, the rear corners of the skull bore little horns.

Gut contents show that *Minmi* was a herbivore that finely chopped its food before swallowing and did not use a gizzard with stomach stones to further process its food.

ID FACT FILE

LENGTH:
16½ ft (2 m)

TIME:
Early Cretaceous

CLASSIFICATION:
Ornithischia
Thyreophora
Ankylosauria

DESCRIPTION:
Medium-sized, heavy bodied quadruped. Body low and broad. A row of flat spikes on each side. Numerous keeled plates on the back and tail.

DIET:
Herbivorous

Hylaeosaurus

(woodland lizard)

Hylaeosaurus was one of the original trio of extinct animals that Richard Owen proposed to call the Dinosauria in 1842. The other two were *Megalosaurus* and *Iguanodon*. Unfortunately, no new remains of *Hylaeosaurus* have come to light since its original discovery, so it has remained a poorly-known beast.

What is known is that it was an ankylosaur, one of the heavily armored four-legged ornithischians.

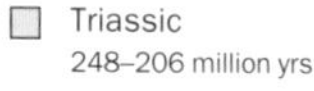

Triassic
248–206 million yrs.

Jurassic
206–144 million yrs.

Cretaceous
144–65 million yrs.

Its armor is not completely known, but we do know that the tail was studded with peaked, oval-shaped horny plates or scutes and that large, flat, triangular spikes protected its flanks. Such lateral spikes are characteristic of both polocanthid and nodosaurid ankylosaurs. No trace of the large shield that occurs over the pelvic region of polacanthids has ever been found, so it is likely that *Hylaeosaurus* did not have one.

Hylaeosaurus is thought to be a primitive nodosaurid. Nodosaurids had narrow beaks and rounded skulls without any horns. They also lacked the tail club of ankylosaurids.

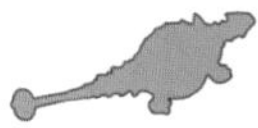

Sauropelta

(lizard skin)

ID FACT FILE

LENGTH:
16½ ft (2 m)

WEIGHT:
2,000 lb (900 kg)

TIME:
Early Cretaceous

CLASSIFICATION:
Ornithischia
Thyreophora
Ankylosauria

DESCRIPTION:
Low, broad body armored with plates: neck and shoulders with a series of large lateral spikes; smaller studs surrounding back and tail. Tail long and flexible.

DIET:
Herbivorous

Sauropelta was a typical nodosaurid ankylosaur. Their skulls were more elongated than other ankylosaurs and had narrower beaks. The downward posture of the skull indicates that *Sauropelta* fed close to ground level, and the narrow beaks suggest that they were more selective browsers than the broad-mouthed grazing ankylosaurids (eg. *Euoplocephalus*, see pp. 120–121).

As in all ankylosaurians, the teeth were minute and only useful for the coarsest

Triassic
248–206 million yrs.

Jurassic
206–144 million yrs.

Cretaceous
144–65 million yrs.

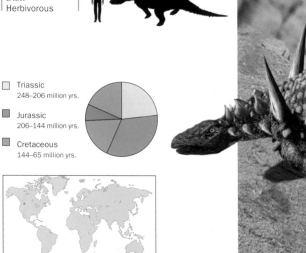

shredding of their food. Much of the food processing would have taken place in the large guts housed in their barrel-shaped bellies. With their large guts and stout limbs, these would not have been speedy animals and would have relied heavily on their armor for protection.

The neck and shoulders of *Sauropelta* were armed with very large conical spikes that would have made it very difficult for a predator to attack from the front. The rest of the back, hips, and tail were covered with a mosaic of keeled plates surrounded by smaller studs. Unlike *Gastonia* (see pp. 118–119), the studs over the hips were not fused into a shield.

ID FACT FILE

LENGTH:
23 ft (7 m)

WEIGHT:
3.5 tons

TIME:
Late Cretaceous

CLASSIFICATION:
Ornithischia
Thyreophora
Ankylosauria

DESCRIPTION:
Large, armored quadruped. Front part of the body armed with large, forward-pointing, lateral spikes, rectangular plates, and smaller studs around back and tail.

DIET:
Herbivorous

Edmontonia

(from Edmonton)

Edmontonia was an advanced nodosaurid. Unlike the earlier *Sauropelta* (see pp. 114–115), it had a complete bony palate separating the mouth cavity from the nasal passages. This would have allowed it to breathe while it was eating. This also would have helped it feed continuously, which it may needed to do if it had a warm-blooded metabolism. Alternatively, it could have lengthened the nasal chambers to improve its sense of smell or to make room for water reclaiming structures.

Triassic
248–206 million yrs.

Jurassic
206–144 million yrs.

Cretaceous
144–65 million yrs.

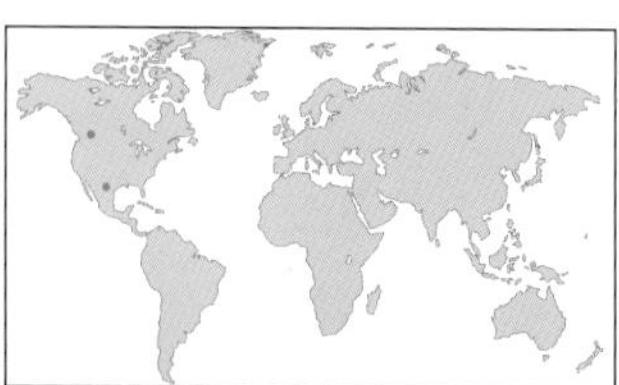

An interesting feature of the armor of *Edmontonia* is that it is concentrated at the font end of its body. This implies that the animal could not have remained passive in the face of an attack. Instead, it would have had to keep moving so that its front end faced the would-be predator. The shoulder spines are particularly massive and point forwards suggesting that *Edmontonia* may have lunged forwards at its attackers.

Gastonia

(named after Robert Gaston)

ID FACT FILE

LENGTH:
16½ ft (5 m)

WEIGHT:
1 ton

TIME:
Early Cretaceous

CLASSIFICATION:
Ornithischia
Thyreophora
Ankylosauria

DESCRIPTION:
Medium-sized, heavy bodied quadruped. Head short and broad with four spikes at its rear corners. Sides of body and tail with a row of flat, triangular spikes. Two rows of tall spikes along the back at the front end of the animal. Hips protected by a shield of fused plates.

DIET:
Herbivorous

This is the best known member of a newly-recognized family of ankylosaurians called polacanthids. Previously polacanthids had been classified with the nodosaurids because they lacked the tail club of ankylosaurids and had large nodosaurid-like lateral spikes.

The discovery of *Gastonia* showed that they had a number of ankylosaurid features such as a skull that is highest in front of the eyes, four triangular horns projecting from its rear corners of the skull, and fused half rings of armor protecting

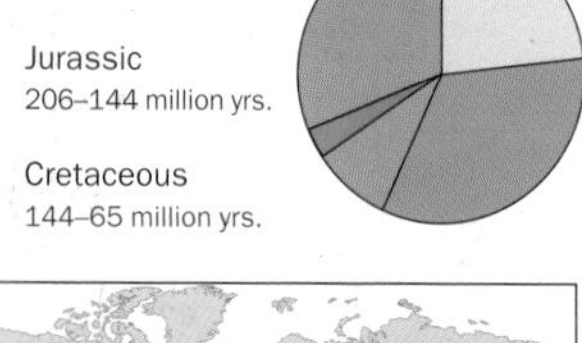

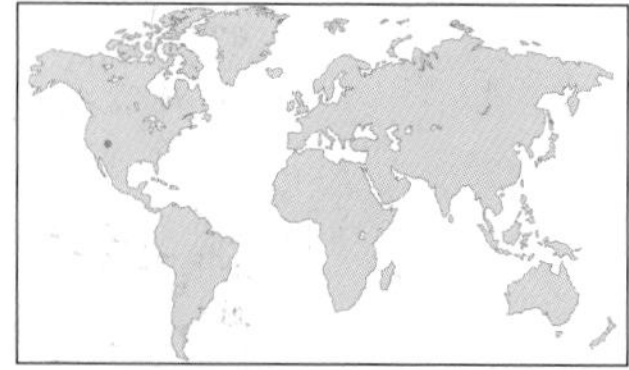

the neck. They are in someway intermediates between the two well-known ankylosaurian families. They also had some peculiar features of their own such as a solidly fused shield of armor covering the hips. *Gastonia* had an additional row of dorsal spikes, each side of the midline, that curved up and out. With so many spikes, *Gastonia* would have been a very difficult animal to approach.

ID FACT FILE

LENGTH:
20 ft (6 m)

WEIGHT:
3 tons

TIME:
Late Cretaceous

CLASSIFICATION:
Ornithischia
Thyreophora
Ankylosauria

DESCRIPTION:
Large, squat, wide-bodied quadruped. Head short and broad with a short horn on each rear corner. Neck protected by fused half-rings of bone. Body covered by bands of bony plates and conical studs. Large pair of studs above shoulders and on tail.

DIET:
Herbivorous

Triassic
248–206 million yrs.

Jurassic
206–144 million yrs.

Cretaceous
144–65 million yrs.

Euoplocephalus

(truly armored head)

Euoplocephalus had one of the most bizarre body shapes of any dinosaur. It had enormous guts held in a very wide abdominal cavity. Add to this a back that was almost as flat as a table, together with short, stumpy legs and you have an animal that would have looked ludicrous in front view.

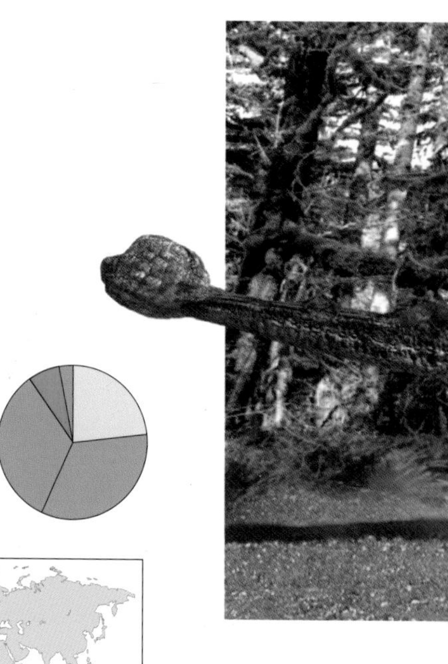

It was heavily armored with bands of small studs set between larger keeled plates and stout spikes. The front half of the tail was similarly armored, but the last half was bare, except for a large, rounded bony club at its tip. There were no large lateral spikes that are present in nodosaurids and polacanthids, but it did share fused half-rings of neck armor with polacanthids. It even had bony eyelids that, when closed, would shield its eyes. This obviously slow animal would have had to rely on its armor to protect it from predators, while using its tail club as a bone-crushing weapon.

ID FACT FILE

LENGTH:
36 ft (11 m)

WEIGHT:
4 tons

TIME:
Late Cretaceous

CLASSIFICATION:
Ornithischia
Thyreophora
Ankylosauria

DESCRIPTION:
Like *Euoplocephalus* but without large conical studs over shoulders, larger horns on the head, and side-facing nostrils.

DIET:
Herbivorous

Triassic
248–206 million yrs.

Jurassic
206–144 million yrs.

Cretaceous
144–65 million yrs.

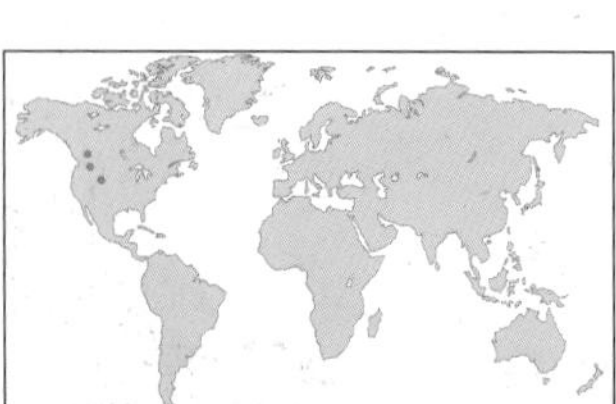

Ankylosaurus

(stiffened lizard)

Like many other dinosaurs (eg. *Anatotitan*, *Tyrannosaurus*, and *Triceratops*) from the very end of the age of Dinosaurs, *Ankylosaurus* was among the largest of its group. It was very similar in overall appearance to *Euoplocephalus* (see pp. 120–121); the main difference being that its nostrils were small and placed on the sides of the snout,

rather than being large and forward facing. In both genera, the internal nasal passages were particularly convoluted and were separated from the mouth cavity by a secondary palate. A secondary palate allowed the animal to continue breathing while food was processed in the mouth, perhaps because it had an elevated metabolism.

Like *Euoplocephalus*, the vertebrae from the last half of the tail interlocked to form a stiff immobile rod, the end of which bore a large, bony club. In contrast, the tail base was quite flexible so that it could wield the end of its tail like a mace.

ID FACT FILE

LENGTH:
10 ft (11 m)

WEIGHT:
165 lb (75 kg)

TIME:
Late Cretaceous

CLASSIFICATION:
Ornithischia, Neornithischia Marginocephalia Pachycephalosauria

DESCRIPTION:
Small biped with a large head and short neck. Skull roof thick, pitted and ornamented. Back of head with a rim of bony knobs. Arms short and slender. Hands unknown. Body, hips, and base of tail very broad. Long stiff tail. Feet with four toes

DIET:
Herbivorous

Triassic
248–206 million yrs.

Jurassic
206–144 million yrs.

Cretaceous
144–65 million yrs.

Homalocephale

(same [-thickness] head)

This dinosaur is a primitive member of the Pachycephalosauria, a group closely related to the Ceratopsia. Like them, these animals have a bony lump on each cheek and a shelf overhanging the back of the head. This shelf was decorated with a row of small knobs.

All pachycephalosaurians, including *Homalocephale*, have thickened skull roofs. However, in *Homalocephale* the skull roof remained flat, rather than bulging into a central dome as it did in

the Pachycephalosauridae. *Homalocephale* is one of the few Pachycephalosaurians for which a relatively complete skeleton is known. Its forelimbs were short and the animal was committed to bipedal locomotion. The ribcage was extremely wide, making room for very enlarged guts and giving the animal an obese appearance. These well-developed guts made up for its small weak teeth, which could do little more than pluck and coarsely shred its leafy food.

ID FACT FILE

LENGTH:
6½ ft (2 m)

WEIGHT:
66 lb (30 kg)

TIME:
Late Cretaceous

CLASSIFICATION:
Ornithischia
Neornithischia
Marginocephalia
Pachycephalosauria

DESCRIPTION:
Small wide-bodied biped. Head large bearing a rounded dome on top of a shelf with small knobs at the rear.

DIET:
Herbivorous

Stegoceras

(roof horn)

This is one of the more common pachycephalosaurians and yet most of the fossils are just the thick skull roofs. Very few complete skulls are known, and only bits and pieces from the rest of the skeleton have been found. The skull roof bulged upwards into a dome of solid bone.

However, unlike more advanced pachycephalosaurids, such as *Pachycephalosaurus* (see pp. 128–129), the dome did

Triassic 248–206 million yrs.

Jurassic 206–144 million yrs.

Cretaceous 144–65 million yrs.

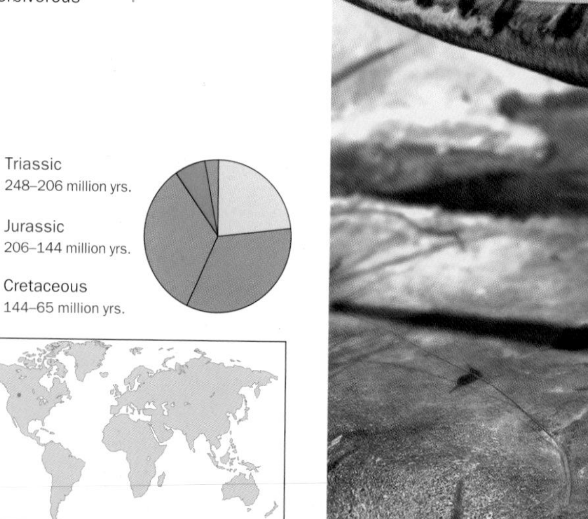

not cover the entire roof of the skull, and the overhanging shelf at the back of the skull remained present.

It also maintained the original upper skull holes of diapsid reptiles, although there were very reduced in size. *Stegoceras* domes come in two distinct types, one quite low and flat, the other quite tall and rounded. These types may correspond to females and males and suggest that some kind of display or combat rituals occurred between *Stegoceras* males.

ID FACT FILE

LENGTH:
Approx. 26 ft (8 m)

TIME:
Late Cretaceous

CLASSIFICATION:
Ornithischia
Neornithischia
Marginocephalia
Pachycephalosauria

DESCRIPTION:
Probably a wide-bodied biped. Skull roof enormously thickened into a dome. Dome extends to the posterior rim of the skull. Roof of snout with a cluster of conical knobs, back of skull with clusters of rounded knobs.

DIET:
Herbivorous

Pachycephalosaurus

(thick-headed lizard)

Pachycephalosaurus was among the last and largest of the dome-headed dinosaur group. Its large dome fully encompassed the bones of the skull roof and obliterated the holes that are usually present at the back of the skull in diapsid reptiles.

The skull was decorated with more knobs and stout spikes than other pachycephalosaurs. These formed clusters around the back of the skull and over the top of the snout.

Triassic
248–206 million yrs.

Jurassic
206–144 million yrs.

Cretaceous
144–65 million yrs.

The microtexture of the bone that forms the dome seems well adapted for coping with large, front-on impact forces.

This supports the hypothesis that the heads were used as battering rams. The animals may have butted heads with each other like modern bighorn sheep do. However, their rounded domes were likely to produce glancing blows. It is more likely that they butted each other on the flanks in territorial battles or butted threatening predators in defense.

ID FACT FILE

LENGTH:
5 ft (1.5 m)

WEIGHT:
33 ft (15 kg)

TIME:
Early Cretaceous

CLASSIFICATION:
Ornithischia
Neornithischia
Marginocephalia
Ceratopsia

DESCRIPTION:
Small, stout biped. Large, short, deep head with parrot-like beak. Sharp cheek projections. Four fingers and toes all with blunt claws.

DIET:
Herbivorous

Psittacosaurus

(parrot lizard)

Psittacosaurus was a small, bipedal ornithischian that, from the neck back, looked like a fat version of *Hypsilophodon* (see pp. 148–149). However, its head betrays its relationship to the giant horned ceratopsians of the Late Cretaceous.

Like all ceratopsians, it had a deep, narrow beak (shaped rather like a parrot's beak) with a unique bone—the rostral

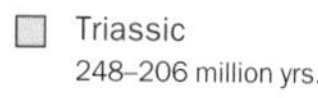

Triassic
248–206 million yrs.

Jurassic
206–144 million yrs.

Cretaceous
144–65 million yrs.

bone—at its tip. The rostral bone is not found anywhere else in the animal kingdom.

It also had a very short shelf-like projection from the back of the head that overhung the articulation between the skull and the neck. In later ceratopsians this shelf would become a large frill.

Several *Psittacosaurus* specimens have been found with clusters of little pebbles preserved in the ribcage. In life these would have been held in a gizzard and would have helped breakdown its food. It is the only ornithischian that is known to have had a gizzard.

ID FACT FILE

Length:
8 ft (2.5 m)

Time:
Late Cretaceous

Classification:
Ornithischia
Neornithischia
Marginocephalia
Ceratopsia

Description:
Small stout quadruped. Head large and deep. Beak parrot-like. Wide shelf projecting back from rear margin of skull. Tail short and deep. Five toes on all feet.

Diet:
Herbivorous

Leptoceratops

(slender-horned face)

This was a very primitive ceratopsian, or horned dinosaur. It had no trace of any facial horns (despite its name), and the shelf at the back of the head (that was to become the frill of later ceratopsians) was only just a little larger than that of *Psittacosaurus* (see pp. 130–131).

Although it had long hindlegs and short, slender forelimbs, it was a quadruped. Its large head and a short tail would have made it too unstable for bipedal locomotion.

Triassic
248–206 million yrs.

Jurassic
206–144 million yrs.

Cretaceous
144–65 million yrs.

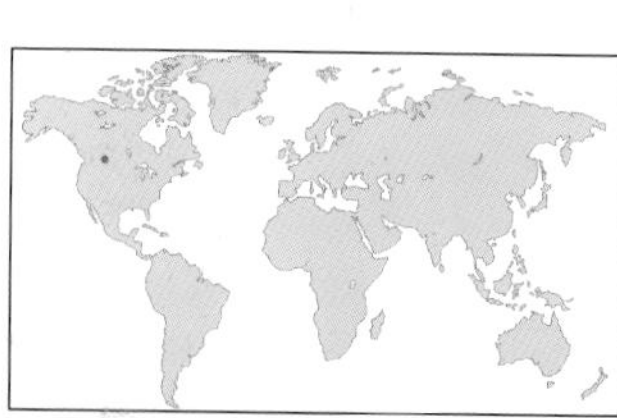

Despite its archaic appearance, it lived right at the end of the age of dinosaurs, alongside such advanced ceratopsians as *Triceratops* (see pp. 146–147). A few features, such as a big gap between the beak and the cheek teeth and fusion between the vertebrae of the neck (to help support the massive head), show that *Leptoceratops* was more closely related to advanced ceratopsians than to the similar-looking *Psittacosaurus*.

Like *Protoceratops* (see pp. 134–135), the vertebral spines of the middle of the tail were extra long and may have supported a low hump.

ID FACT FILE

LENGTH:
10 ft (3 m)

WEIGHT:
121 lb (55 kg)

TIME:
Late Cretaceous

CLASSIFICATION:
Ornithischia
Neornithischia
Marginocephalia
Ceratopsia

DESCRIPTION:
Small stout quadruped. Head large with deep parrot-like beak. Rear margin of skull with a short frill. Five toes on all feet. Short, leaf-shaped tail.

DIET:
Herbivorous

Triassic
248–206 million yrs.

Jurassic
206–144 million yrs.

Cretaceous
144–65 million yrs.

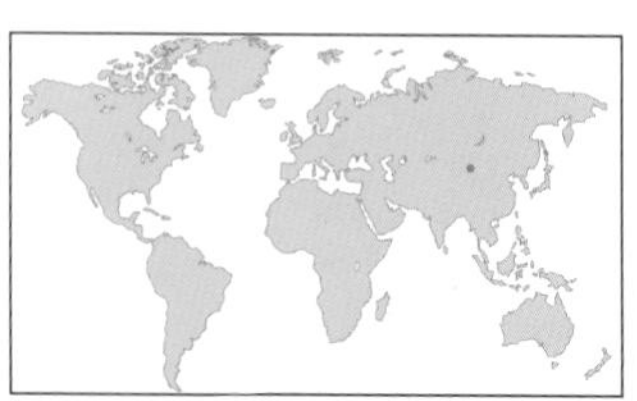

Protoceratops

(before the horned face)

When this dinosaur was first described, it was immediately obvious that it was a link between the large horned ceratopsids and more primitive ornithischians.

Like ceratopsids, it was a large-headed four-legged animal. The most obvious specialization it shared with the ceratopsids was the extension of the rear margin of the skull into a frill that covered the neck. However, it lacked the impressive facial horns of true ceratopsids, although large

individuals (presumably males) did grow a sharp, pointed bump over their noses. Another primitive feature was the group of teeth in the front of the upper jaw.

Protoceratops lived in desert-like conditions, and its remains are frequently found buried in wind-blown, sand dune deposits. The spines of the tail vertebrae are extra tall and may have supported a camel-like water, or food, storing hump. For many years, the eggs of *Oviraptor* (see pp. 212–213) were mistakenly thought to belong to *Protoceratops*.

ID FACT FILE

Length:
18 ft (5.5 m)

Time:
Late Cretaceous

Classification:
Ornithischia
Neornithischia
Marginocephalia
Ceratopsia

Description:
Large heavy bodied quadruped. Head narrow and deep. Deep parrot-like beak. Long horn over the nose and smaller horns over the eyes. Short frill with three six large horns and two smaller horns on its margin. Short sprawled forelegs. All feet with five short toes, blunt claw-like hoofs. Tail short.

Diet:
Herbivorous

Triassic
248–206 million yrs.

Jurassic
206–144 million yrs.

Cretaceous
144–65 million yrs.

Styracosaurus

(spiked lizard)

The latest Cretaceous of North America saw the flowering of the most advanced family of Ceratopsians, the ceratopsids themselves.

Unlike earlier ceratopsians, these animals grew impressive horns on their faces and kept a battery of continually growing teeth in their jaws. In this respect their teeth converged upon those of the hadrosaurids, but unlike these dinosaurs, ceratopsids'

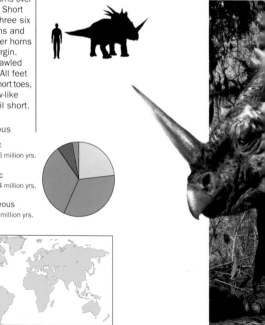

dental batteries formed a set of shearing blades for slicing up food rather than grinding it.

Nevertheless, it is clear that they were vegetarians. There are two main groups of ceratopsids, the long-frilled group and the short frilled group. *Styracosaurus* was a member of the short frilled group, which (apart from frill size) were characterized by a long nasal horn and short brow horns.

Styracosaurus was distinctive in that a group of six long horns grew back from the rear margin of its frill, giving it a very spiky appearance!

ID FACT FILE

LENGTH:
20 ft (6 m)

WEIGHT:
2 tons

TIME:
Late Cretaceous

CLASSIFICATION:
Ornithischia
Neornithischia
Marginocephalia
Ceratopsia

DESCRIPTION:
Head narrow and deep. Deep parrot-like beak. Broad nasal horn that was strongly bent forward. Small, irregular horns over the eyes. Short frill with two large horns on its rear margin. Body as in *Styracosaurus*.

DIET:
Herbivorous

Einiosaurus

(bison lizard)

Einiosaurus was a fairly typical short-frilled ceratopsid. It was distinctive in having a wide but flat nasal horn that curved forward over the tip of the snout.

Growth series show that this unusual shape grew as the animal got older. The nasal horn of a juvenile resembled an adult's in being wide and flat, but it was also erect and did not curve forward. Adult *Einiosaurus* also had a single pair of long horns projecting back from the

Triassic
248–206 million yrs.

Jurassic
206–144 million yrs.

Cretaceous
144–65 million yrs.

posterior rim of its frill, a feature shared with *Pachyrhinosaurus* (see pp. 140–141).

Like many ceratopsids, *Einiosaurus* also had horns over each eye, but these were low and irregular in shape. The remains of many individuals have been found together in a bonebed suggesting that a herd of *Einiosaurus* had been killed. The distinctive patterns of horns—which each type of ceratopsid displays—were probably used as species recognition structures, much like the crests of hadrosaurids, and would be useful for herd formation.

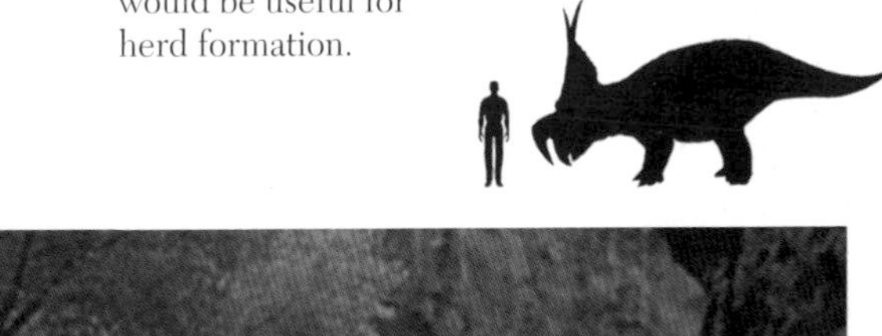

ID FACT FILE

LENGTH:
23 ft (7 m)

TIME:
Late Cretaceous

CLASSIFICATION:
Ornithischia
Neornithischia
Marginocephalia
Ceratopsia

DESCRIPTION:
Head large. Deep parrot-like beak. Broad flat pad on snout. Smaller pads over eyes. Short frill. Two sideways pointing horns on frill margin. Three short horns in center of frill. Body as in *Stryracosaurus*.

DIET:
Herbivorous

Pachyrhinosaurus

(thick-nosed lizard)

This was the largest short-frilled ceratopsid. It had replaced its facial horns with large bony bosses that were probably covered by horny pads in life. The nasal boss was particularly large and formed a large, flat, pad that dominated the face.

Like the dome of pachycephalosaurs, the nasal pad could have been used in butting contests. However, the

Triassic
248–206 million yrs.

Jurassic
206–144 million yrs.

Cretaceous
144–65 million yrs.

frill remained spiky with a large horn jutting out on each side and a cluster of three small horns placed in the center of the frill.

Its remains have been found in far northern North America. These northerly sites would have been well within the Cretaceous Arctic Circle. This has led to suggestions that herds of *Pachyrhinosaurus* migrated in and out of the Arctic each year. However there is no evidence for such a migration, and it is possible that they simply stayed and withstood the Arctic winter.

ID FACT FILE

Length:
16½ ft (5 m)

Weight:
1.7 tons

Time:
Late Cretaceous

Classification:
Ornithischia
Neornithischia
Marginocephalia
Ceratopsia

Description:
Head narrow and deep. Deep parrot-like beak. Moderately large, erect, nasal horn. Backward-curved horn of variable size over each eye. Long rectangular frill. Frill margin with triangular studs. Extra large studs on the rear corners of the frill. Body as in *Styracosaurus*.

Diet:
Herbivorous

Chasmosaurus

(chasm lizard)

This was a typical long frilled ceratopsid. Its face was armored with a short nose horn and two backward-curving brow horns. The size of the brow horns was variable. In some they were much longer than the nose horn (like *Triceratops*, see pp. 146–147) while in others they were no bigger than the nose horn.

This may represent a sexual difference. The frill of *Chasmosaurus* was quite tall

Triassic
248–206 million yrs.

Jurassic
206–144 million yrs.

Cretaceous
144–65 million yrs.

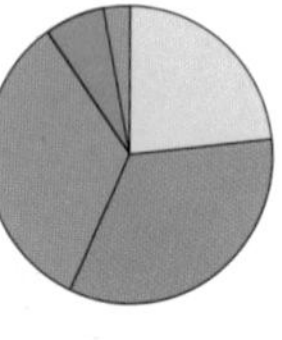

and erect and was long enough to cover the shoulders when the head was lifted.

The frill was pierced by windows that were so big that they reduced the bony part of the frill into a light series of connected struts. The margins of the frill were decorated with pointed triangular bones with particularly large ones at the rear corners of the frill.

Like many dinosaurs, the nasal chambers of ceratopsids, including *Chasmosaurus*, were greatly enlarged.

ID FACT FILE

LENGTH:
26 ft (8 m)

WEIGHT:
5 tons

TIME:
Late Cretaceous

CLASSIFICATION:
Ornithischia
Neornithischia
Marginocephalia
Ceratopsia

DESCRIPTION:
Head narrow and deep. Deep parrot-like beak. Small nasal horn. Very large forward pointing horns over each eye. Frill very long with smooth margins. Body as in *Styracosaurus*.

DIET:
Herbivorous

Torosaurus

(perforated lizard)

Torosaurus has the distinction of having the largest skull of any known terrestrial animal. One skull measures 7½ ft (2.3 m) in length. Much of this length is taken up by a very long frill, which—unlike other ceratopsids—had smooth margins.

As with other ceratopsids, it was probably sexually dimorphic. There exist two types of skulls: a large one with erect brow horns and a smaller variety with forward pointing brow horns.

Torosaurus also had a short, conical nasal horn. It was a contemporary of *Triceratops* (see pp. 146–147), but its

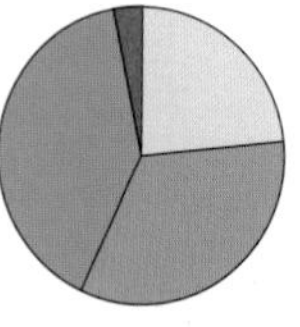

fossils are much less common. A recently-discovered forelimb of *Torosaurus* has helped resolve the debate over the posture of the forelimbs of ceratopsids.

It has shown that, unlike the erect hindlimbs, the forelimbs were held in a semi-sprawled position with the elbows bowed outwards and that the forefeet were planted further from the midline than the hindfeet. The significance of this unusual posture is not understood at present.

Triceratops

(three-horned face)

ID FACT FILE

LENGTH:
30 ft (9 m)

WEIGHT:
6 tons

TIME:
Late Cretaceous

CLASSIFICATION:
Ornithischia
Neornithischia
Marginocephalia
Ceratopsia

DESCRIPTION:
Same as Torosaurus but with a short, rounded frill bordered with triangular studs.

DIET:
Herbivorous

A classic and much loved dinosaur, *Triceratops* is often used as the typical example of a ceratopsian dinosaur. Nevertheless, it was quite unusual for the group. It had the typical long brow horns and short nasal horn of a long frilled ceratopsid, but its frill was short.

Its frill was also unlike both long and short frilled ceratopsids in being solid and lacking large holes to reduce its weight. Enough similarities between *Triceratops* and long frilled ceratopsids exist to demonstrate that

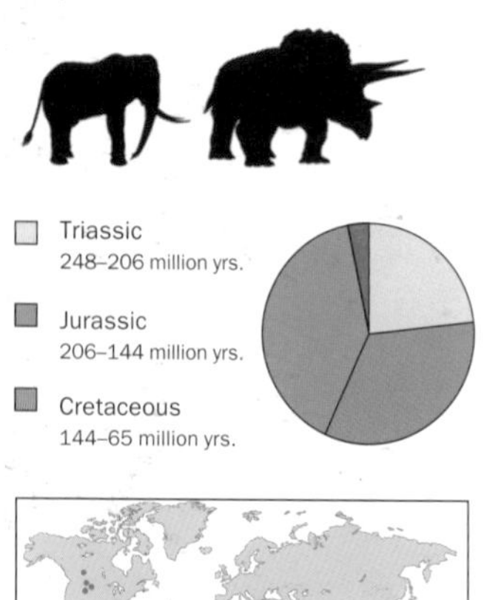

it is a member of the long frilled group that had evolved an unusual frill. Like most ceratopsids, the margins of the frill were decorated with little pointed studs. Its large horns were clearly dangerous weapons that would have helped protect it against predators. They could have also been used in battles with other *Triceratops* over territories or mates, much like modern horned mammals do.

ID FACT FILE

LENGTH:
4 ft (1.4 m)

WEIGHT:
22 lb (10 kg)

TIME:
Early Cretaceous

CLASSIFICATION:
Ornithischia
Neornithischia
Ornithopoda

DESCRIPTION:
Medium sized, lightly-built, biped with a small short skull. Arms short with four blunt-clawed fingers and feet with four toes.

DIET:
Herbivorous

Hypsilophodon

(high-ridge tooth)

Despite living in the last period of the Mesozoic Era, *Hypsilophodon* was a primitive ornithischian that would have resembled the common ancestor of the whole group.

Like the ancestral ornithischians, it was a small, light-weight biped. Its head was short with a pointed beak, which retained a row of teeth in the upper part. It also had four digits on both hands and feet.

Triassic
248–206 million yrs.

Jurassic
206–144 million yrs.

Cretaceous
144–65 million yrs.

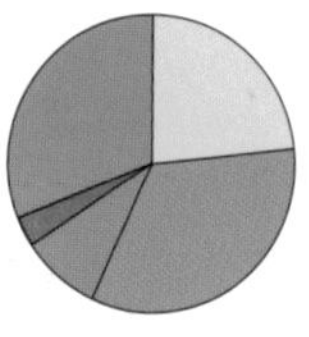

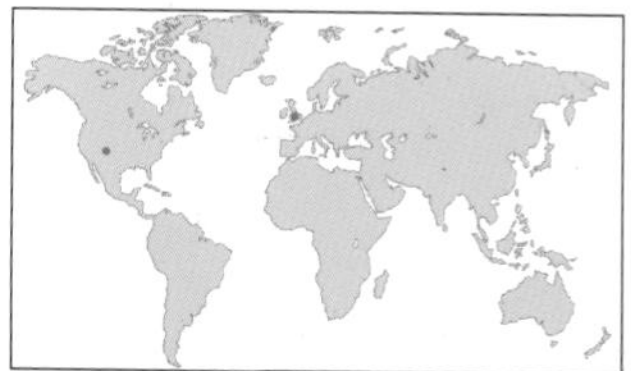

Nevertheless, some more subtle aspects of its anatomy showed that it was had changed somewhat from the ancestral condition. Its teeth were inset well away from the edge of the jaws, creating a space that probably formed cheek pouches in life. The enamel of its teeth was also thicker on one side so that when they were worn down, it formed a cutting edge.

These are herbivorous specializations that are present in the earliest ornithischians. It was a small and fleet-footed animal, rather like the gazelle of its day.

ID FACT FILE

LENGTH:
6½ ft (2 m)

TIME:
Early Cretaceous

CLASSIFICATION:
Ornithischia
Neornithischia
Ornithopoda

DESCRIPTION:
As far as we know the same as *Hypsilophodon*, though possibly with larger eyes.

DIET:
Herbivorous

Leaellynasaura

(Leaellyn's lizard)

Leaellynasaura was very similar to *Hypsilophodon*, differing only in having ridges on both sides of the teeth (as opposed to solely on the outside) and in having a flatter lower end of the thigh bone (femur). *Laellynasaura* lived in Southern Australia during the Early Cretaceous when it was well in the Antarctic Circle.

Although the Earth's climate was a lot milder then, there is still evidence that temperatures dropped below freezing during

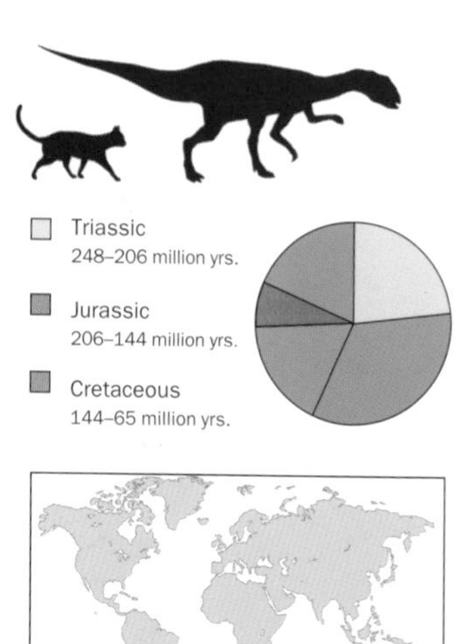

the long, dark winters. Even more surprising is that the microtexture of their bones indicate that they grew quickly and continuously to adult size. In a harsh climate this could only be achieved through a "warm-blooded" metabolism.

The only known skull is a juvenile; it has large eyes and well-developed optic lobes in its brain cavity. Some have suggested that the large eyes helped it to see during the dark polar winter, but they are typical features of a juvenile animal.

ID FACT FILE

LENGTH:
16½ ft (5 m)

WEIGHT:
660 lb (300 kg)

TIME:
Early Cretaceous

CLASSIFICATION:
Ornithischia
Neornithischia
Ornithopoda
Iguanodontia

DESCRIPTION:
Medium sized, heavily built biped or quadruped with a moderately large, deep skull. Hands with three clawed fingers, fourth and fifth finger clawless stumps. Feet with four toes. Tail very long.

DIET:
Herbivorous

Tenontosaurus

(tendon lizard)

The long tail of this dinosaur took up much of its length. Although moderately large, and possibly four-legged, this animal shares many similarities with the small, bipedal *Hypsilophodon*. Some palaeontologists believe that it was a giant hypsilophodontid and should not be classified in the Iguanodontia.

Nevertheless, like *Dryosaurus* (see pp. 44–45), it had no teeth at the front of its jaws and had a deep groove in its thigh

Triassic
248–206 million yrs.

Jurassic
206–144 million yrs.

Cretaceous
144–65 million yrs.

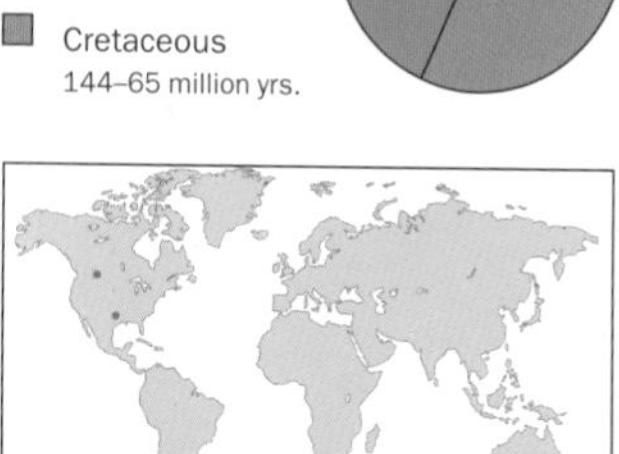

bone for strong leg muscles, so it is probably a primitive iguanodontian.

Tenontosaurus was a common herbivore in its time and place and appears to have been a favorite prey animal of *Deinonychus* (see pp. 222–223). One skeleton was found together with a number of *Deinonychus* skeletons. Perhaps these were unlucky members of a pack that were killed by the struggling *Tenontosaurus* before it was finally brought down.

ID FACT FILE

LENGTH:
30 ft (9 m)

WEIGHT:
4 tons

TIME:
Early Cretaceous

CLASSIFICATION:
Ornithischia
Neornithischia
Ornithopoda
Iguanodontia

DESCRIPTION:
Large,heavy-bodied biped. Large head with toothless beak at front and inflated nasal chamber on snout. Neck moderately long. Arms long. Probably five fingers. Three short toes

DIET:
Herbivorous

Muttaburrasaurus

(lizard from Muttaburra)

Muttaburrasaurus is one of the few Australian dinosaurs known from a largely complete skeleton. It was a large, heavy-bodied plant eater that superficially resembled *Iguanodon* (see pp. 156–157).

Nevertheless, many aspects of its anatomy show that, among the iguanodontians, it was not a particularly close relative of Iguanodon. Instead *Muttaburrasaurus* may be a member of an endemic Australian family that we know

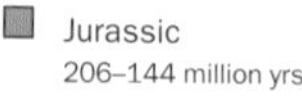

Triassic
248–206 million yrs.

Jurassic
206–144 million yrs.

Cretaceous
144–65 million yrs.

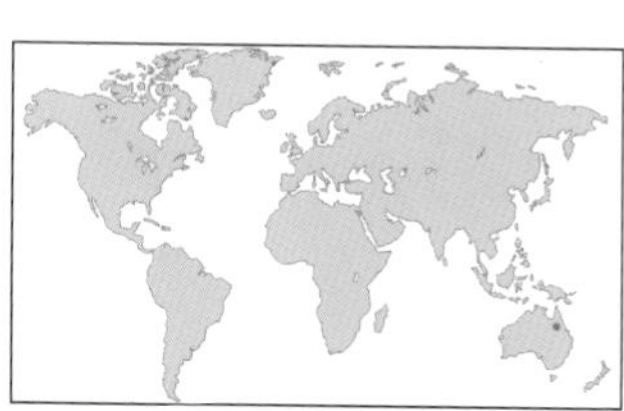

little about. *Muttaburrasaurus* certainly has a number of features that make it quite distinct among iguanodontians. Most striking were the inflated nasal chambers that produced a dorsal bulge along the profile of the snout. These may have functioned as resonating chambers to produce a loud call, or they may have warmed up inspired air.

Another intriguing aspect was its enlarged jaw closing muscles and its teeth, which formed scissor-like shearing blades. Like a ceratopsian dinosaur, it may have chopped its food up rather than grinding it, as did other iguanodontians.

ID FACT FILE

LENGTH:
36 ft (11 m)

WEIGHT:
5.5 tons

TIME:
Early Cretaceous

CLASSIFICATION:
Ornithischia
Neornithischia
Ornithopoda
Iguanodontia

DESCRIPTION:
Large, heavy-bodied. Long head with toothless beak. Forelegs smaller than hindlegs. Forefeet with large spike, central digits in a single unit, small grasping inner digit.

DIET:
Herbivorous

Iguanodon

(iguana tooth)

This was a common and widespread herbivore in the Early Cretaceous. It has been found in North America and Asia, but it is in Europe where it is very common, making up most of the Early Cretaceous dinosaur finds of that continent. It is not surprising then that some of the earliest dinosaur finds belonged to this dinosaur.

It was a large iguanodontian that had developed long strong forelimbs. In all

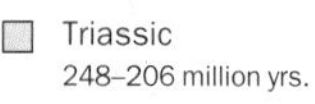

Triassic
248–206 million yrs.

Jurassic
206–144 million yrs.

Cretaceous
144–65 million yrs.

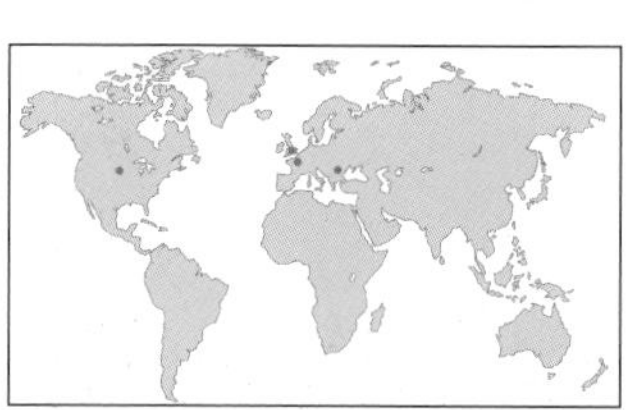

probability the animal had become a quadruped, but it would have been capable of some bipedal locomotion.

The thumb had been transformed into a large, conical spike that would have made a dangerous offensive weapon. The middle digits of the hand supported the weight of the animal, while the fifth digit formed a slender and flexible finger that could grasp vegetation and bring to the mouth. Only three toes with blunt claws remained on the stocky hindleg.

ID FACT FILE

LENGTH:
20 ft (6 m)

WEIGHT:
1 ton

TIME:
Early Cretaceous

CLASSIFICATION:
Ornithischia
Neornithischia
Ornithopoda
Iguanodontia

DESCRIPTION:
Large, heavy-bodied. Tall sail or narrow hump over body, hips, and tail. Forelegs smaller than hindlegs. Forefeet with small spike and grasping inner digit.

DIET:
Herbivorous

Ouranosaurus

(brave lizard)

This dinosaur was found in the sands of the Sahara desert. Of course at the time of burial the desert did not exist and there was plenty of vegetation and fresh water.

Nevertheless, it was a tropical place and during the Cretaceous the days could have got very hot. This may give some clue to the function of the most distinctive feature of *Ouranosaurus*, the tall crest running along its back.

Triassic
248–206 million yrs.

Jurassic
206–144 million yrs.

Cretaceous
144–65 million yrs.

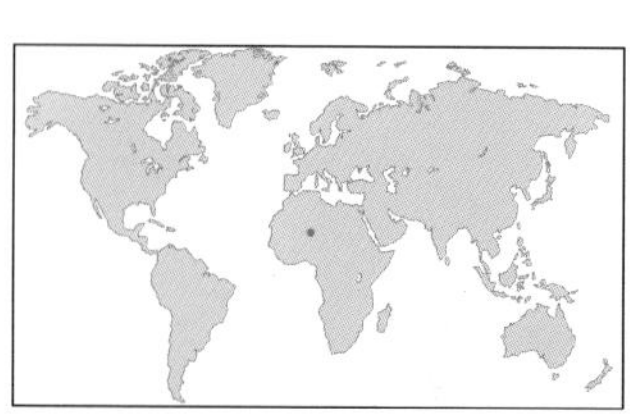

This crest was formed from enormously elongated spines growing out of the top of each of its trunk vertebrae. Usually, these are reconstructed as supporting a skin-covered sail, but a large fatty hump is equally plausible. A sail could act as a radiator to help cool the animal, whereas a hump could insulate the torso from the overhead sun as well as store fat reserves.

Like the hadrosaurids, *Ouranosaurus* had a broad duck-like beak for cropping plants.

ID FACT FILE

LENGTH:
30 ft (9 m)

TIME:
Late Cretaceous

CLASSIFICATION:
Ornithischia
Neornithischia
Ornithopoda
Iguanodontia

DESCRIPTION:
Large, heavy quadruped. Large hump on snout above nose. Forelimbs shorter and slimmer than hindlimbs. Serrated frill of skin on back. Moderately short, straight, deep tail.

DIET:
Herbivorous

Gryposaurus

(hook [-nosed] lizard)

The Hadrosauridae was the dominant family of plant eaters in the Northern Hemisphere of the Late Cretaceous. They differ from other iguanodontians in lacking a thumb—or thumbspike—and in having batteries of small teeth, all tightly packed together with old, worn teeth being continually replaced by new teeth growing from underneath. In this way the teeth formed a single, large, grinding surface in each jaw, which was maintained at all times.

Triassic
248–206 million yrs.

Jurassic
206–144 million yrs.

Cretaceous
144–65 million yrs.

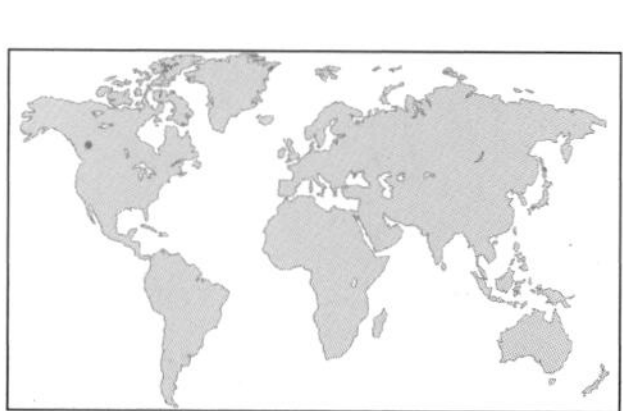

Hadrosaurids also had broad and toothless beaks in front of their dental batteries, which has given them their nickname: duckbilled dinosaurs.

Many hadrosaurids had crests adorning their heads, although *Gryposaurus* did not. It did have a swollen bump over the top of its large nostrils. An even larger depression encircling the nostrils suggests that in life there was a very large outer nasal chamber that was covered by soft tissues. Although it is not known for sure, it may have formed a resonating chamber that gave it a loud and distinctive voice when calling to other *Gryposaurus*.

ID FACT FILE

LENGTH:
10 ft (13 m)

WEIGHT:
7.5 tons

TIME:
Late Cretaceous

CLASSIFICATION:
Ornithischia
Neornithischia
Ornithopoda
Iguanodontia

DESCRIPTION:
Like *Gryposaurus* but with a longer lower head. No nasal hump and a wider beak.

DIET:
Herbivorous

Anatotitan

(duck giant)

Anatotitan was a very large hadrosaurid from the latest Cretaceous of North America. It was a contemporary of *Tyrannosaurus* (see pp. 196–197), and almost certainly fell prey to it on many occasions.

It was a crestless hadrosaurid with a long, flattened skull. Its beak was very broad and particularly duck-like. Far from being used to dabble in ponds, its broad beak,

Triassic
248–206 million yrs.

Jurassic
206–144 million yrs.

Cretaceous
144–65 million yrs.

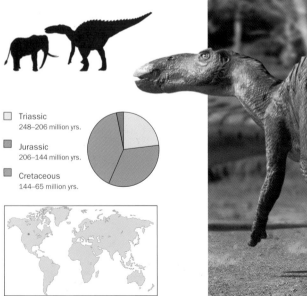

with its sharp cutting edge would have been used for cropping large amounts of low growing vegetation. Modern grazing herbivores also have broad mouths for cropping a lot of food in each mouthful. A mummified *Anatotitan*, with the contents of its stomach preserved, proved that it fed on land plants.

Like other hadrosaurids, *Anatotitan* had a deep flattened tail. This tail looks like a good sculling organ for an aquatic animal, but close examination shows that it was poorly muscled and was held stiff by a lattice of bony tendons. Thus, the deep tail may have been a display organ or possibly a fat storage area.

ID FACT FILE

LENGTH:
30 ft (9 m)

WEIGHT:
4 tons

TIME:
Late Cretaceous

CLASSIFICATION:
Ornithischia
Neornithischia
Ornithopoda
Iguanodontia

DESCRIPTION:
Long head with broad beak and a small, pointed crest above eyes. Body the same as Gryposaurus.

DIET:
Herbivorous

Maiasaura

(mother lizard)

Maisaura was a hadrosaurid that lived on the upper coastal plain of western North America in the Late Cretaceous. We know more about the biology of this dinosaur than almost any other, thanks to a series of remarkable discoveries by palaeontologist John Horner. One of these discoveries was a nesting ground complete with eggs and babies.

Many *Maiasaura* congregated to build scooped-out mounds of mud into which they laid their eggs. We know from the

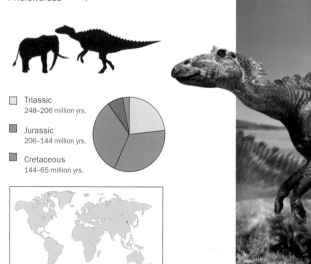

Triassic
248–206 million yrs.

Jurassic
206–144 million yrs.

Cretaceous
144–65 million yrs.

baby bones buried in these mounds that the young stayed in the nest while the parents bought food to them. This parental care can be proved by the fact that the baby skeletons in the nest were 2–3 times as big as the eggs, and so must have grown in the nest for a certain period after hatching.

Another staggering discovery was a bonebed produced when a massive herd, estimated to have contained 10,000 *Maiasaura*, was killed by a volcanic eruption. It seems that *Maisaura* may have migrated annually in herds along the upper coastal plain. Apart from this, it was a relatively plain looking solid-crested hadrosaurid whose crest was a simple low ridge above its eyes.

ID FACT FILE

LENGTH:
36 ft (11 m)

WEIGHT:
5.5 tons

TIME:
Late Cretaceous

CLASSIFICATION:
Ornithischia
Neornithischia
Ornithopoda
Iguanodontia

DESCRIPTION:
Long head with broad beak. Long pointed spike projecting backwards from between the eyes. Body the same as *Gryposaurus.*

DIET:
Herbivorous

Saurolophus

(lizard crest)

Saurolophus was one of the solid-crested hadrosaurids, as were *Anatotitan* (see pp. 162–163) and *Gryposaurus* (see pp. 160–161).

Saurolophus had a solid, bony spike projected up and back from the top of its head. The depressions that surround the bony nostrils of the skull extend up onto this spike, suggesting that in life it supported an enlarged nasal chamber. Perhaps this chamber formed an

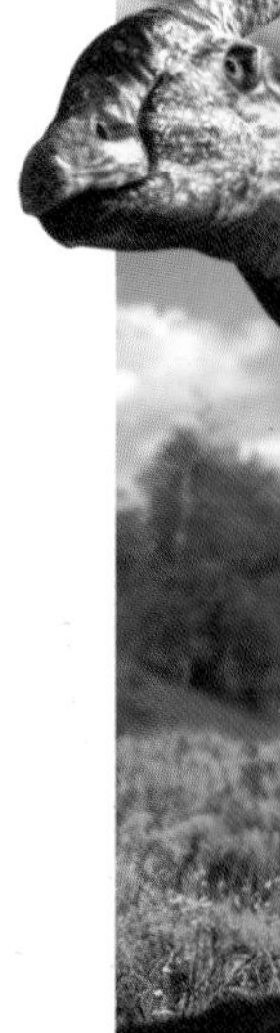

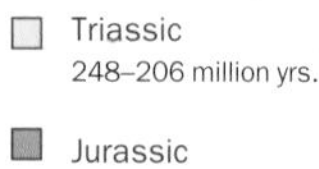

inflatable sac that, when blown up, could act as a resonating chamber that would produce a very load call.

Saurolophus is interesting as it is found in both Western North America and Eastern Asia. This distribution provides evidence that a land-bridge across the Bering Sea existed at some point in the Late Cretaceous, allowing animals to cross from one continent to the other. In Asia, it would have formed the main food source of the tyrannosaurid *Tarbosaurus* (see pp. 194–195).

ID FACT FILE

LENGTH:
30 ft (9 m)

WEIGHT:
4 tons

TIME:
Late Cretaceous

CLASSIFICATION:
Ornithischia
Neornithischia
Ornithopoda
Iguanodontia

DESCRIPTION:
Short deep head with narrow beak. Long thick, tube-like crest curving over neck from the back of the head. Body deep. Back bent strongly downwards towards the neck. Tall, fleshy ridge on top of back and tail.

DIET:
Herbivorous

Triassic
248–206 million yrs.

Jurassic
206–144 million yrs.

Cretaceous
144–65 million yrs.

Parasaurolophus

(beside Saurolophus)

Parasaurolophus was a member of the second major group of hadrosaurids: the hollow crested forms. As the name suggests, the head crests of the hadrosaurids were hollowed out by large, tortuous nasal passages. A number of functions have been suggested for these, but the only idea that seems feasible was that they were used as resonating chambers to produce a distinctive call (like the pipes of a trombone). Such calls

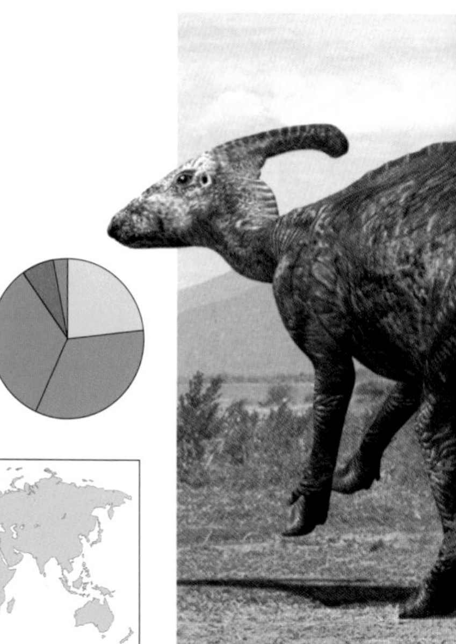

would have been very useful for social interactions. There is ample evidence that hadrosaurids were herding creatures.

Its crest was a large cylindrical structure, extending back over the neck, that could exceed in length the rest of the head. Some specimens have a much shorter and tightly curved crest; these may well have been females. Hollow crested hadrosaurids had particularly long, robust forelimbs and probably walked on four legs for most of the time.

ID FACT FILE

LENGTH:
33 ft (10 m)

TIME:
Late Cretaceous

CLASSIFICATION:
Ornithischia
Neornithischia
Ornithopoda
Iguanodontia

DESCRIPTION:
As in *Parasaurolophus* except with a semicircular plate-like crest on top of the head. Ribbon-like skin frill on the back and tail.

DIET:
Herbivorous

Corythosaurus

(helmeted lizard)

The hollow crest of *Corythosaurus* formed a large, rounded crest over the top of its head which in profile resembled a helmet, hence the name. Like other hollow crested forms, the crest appears to have varied between the sexes with the probable females having a smaller narrow crest than the males. Hatchlings of a close relative, *Hypacrosaurus*, show that the young had no crest and that it developed as the animal got older.

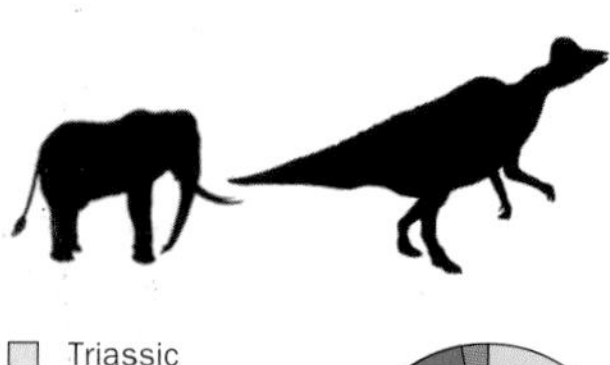

Triassic
248–206 million yrs.

Jurassic
206–144 million yrs.

Cretaceous
144–65 million yrs.

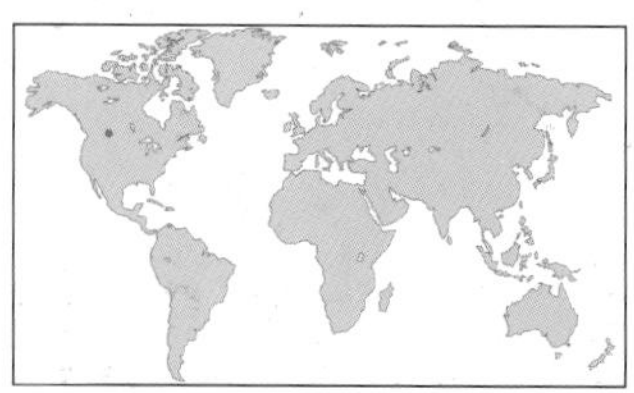

Another feature in common with other hollow crested hadrosaurids is the relatively narrow beak compared to those of crestless, and solid crested, hadrosaurids. This indicates that these animals were more choosy feeders, probably plucking at the more nutritious leaves rather than biting off large swathes of vegetation with each bite.

Excellent skin impressions have been found surrounding a *Corythosaurus* skeleton. These show that the skin was covered in a mosaic of large polygonal scales and that there was a soft frill extending along the length of the back and tail.

ID FACT FILE

LENGTH:
50 ft (15 m)

TIME:
Late Cretaceous

CLASSIFICATION:
Ornithischia
Neornithischia
Ornithopoda
Iguanodontia

DESCRIPTION:
As in Parasaurolophus except with a forward pointing tongue-shaped crest and a backwards pointing crest on top of head.

DIET:
Herbivorous

Lambeosaurus

(Lambe's lizard)

Lambeosaurus was a hollow-crested hadrosaurid, closely related to *Corythosaurus*. It differed from that genus in having a tongue-shaped crest that leaned forward over the snout and a solid prong projecting back from the base of the crest.

Growth series of this dinosaur exist and show that the crest started out as a small bump in juveniles, which then enlarged as the animal grew.

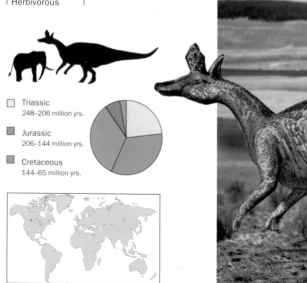

Triassic
248–206 million yrs.

Jurassic
206–144 million yrs.

Cretaceous
144–65 million yrs.

Female crests were not as large as those of the males. Thus it seems the external shape of the crest was an excellent marker of an individuals' species, age, and sex. Thus, the crests would have played an important role in social interactions, which would have been important for these herd-forming dinosaurs.

All hollow-crested hadrosaurids had tall spines atop their vertebrae, which produced a tall ridge along their backs and a particularly deep tail. These features were especially well developed in *Lambeosaurus*.

ID FACT FILE

LENGTH:
33 ft (10 m)

WEIGHT:
7 tons

TIME:
Early Cretaceous

CLASSIFICATION:
Saurischia
Sauropodomorpha
Sauropoda
Neosauropoda

DESCRIPTION:
Large quadruped with columnar limbs. Head with long, low and wide snout. Head pointing down or back. Moderately long neck that was bent downward Neck with 12 pairs of tall spines. Forelimbs shorter than hindlimbs. High ridge over back and tail. Long tail.

DIET:
Herbivorous

Triassic
248–206 million yrs.

Jurassic
206–144 million yrs.

Cretaceous
144–65 million yrs.

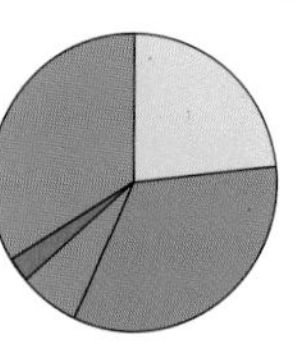

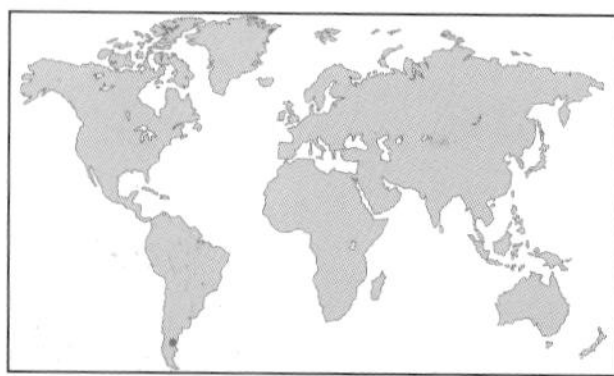

Amargasaurus

(lizard from La Amarga [Canyon])

It is becoming clear that the well-known dinosaur faunas of the Cretaceous North America and Asia were not typical of the rest of the world. For instance, we now know that sauropods did not dwindle towards extinction, but continued to flourish on other continents during the Cretaceous.

Amargasaurus was one of these. It was related to *Diplodocus* (see pp. 58–59), but looked very different. Instead of having a long, flexible neck, its neck was shorter and was bent steeply downward, so that the head would have been carried close to the ground.

Thus, it seems *Amargasurus* was a sauropod that grazed upon the vegetation that covered the ground. Adding to its bizarre appearance was a tall, thick ridge running over its back and hips. Most unusual of all were the pairs of long spines that projected from the top of each vertebra of the neck. These spines formed two parallel rows along the top of the neck. The function of these spines remains unknown.

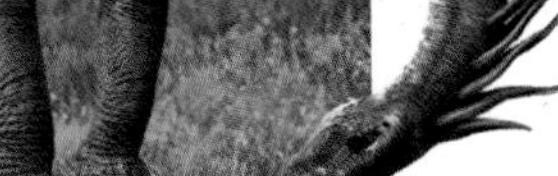

Nemegtosaurus

(lizard from the Nemegt)

Most sauropod skeletons are found without a skull because the small delicate head is easily destroyed by erosion or scavenging.

Nemegtosaurus is the complete opposite; it is only known from an isolated skull. It also comes from a time and place where sauropods are rare and poorly known, making it very difficult to determine what kind of sauropod it really was.

ID FACT FILE

LENGTH:
40 ft (12 m)

TIME:
Late Cretaceous

CLASSIFICATION:
Saurischia
Sauropodomorpha
Sauropoda
Neosauropoda

DESCRIPTION:
Body unknown, almost certainly a large quadruped with columnar limbs and a long neck. Head long, low, and broad. Nostrils above eyes. Pencil-shaped teeth at front of jaws only.

DIET:
Herbivorous

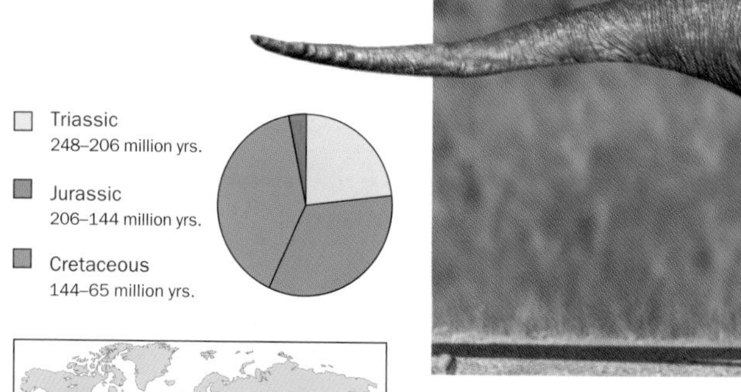

The skull broadly resembles that of *Diplodocus* (see pp. 58–59), especially with its peg-like teeth restricted to the very front of its jaws. However, it is known that titanosaurids (eg. *Saltasaurus*, pp. 178–179) had evolved peg-like teeth as a convergence with diplodocids, and some of the features of *Nemegtosaurus* are titanosaurid-like.

If *Nemegtosaurus* really is a titanosaurid, then it might belong to the headless titanosaurid skeleton called *Opisthocoelocaudia* (The name is quite a mouthful!), known from the same rock formation. The reconstruction presented here is based on this idea.

ID FACT FILE

Length:
40 ft (12 m)

Time:
Late Cretaceous

Classification:
Saurischia
Sauropodomorpha
Sauropoda
Neosauropoda

Description:
Heavy bodied quadruped with columnar limbs. Moderately long neck. Wide barrel-shaped body with level back. Armored with large keeled plates and smaller studs. Forefeet with no toes or claws. Hindfeet with five toes and three claws.

Diet:
Herbivorous

Triassic
248–206 million yrs.

Jurassic
206–144 million yrs.

Cretaceous
144–65 million yrs.

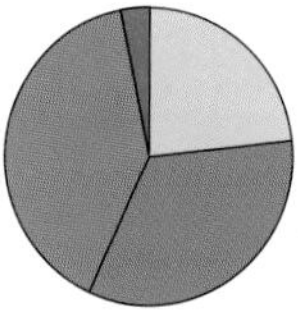

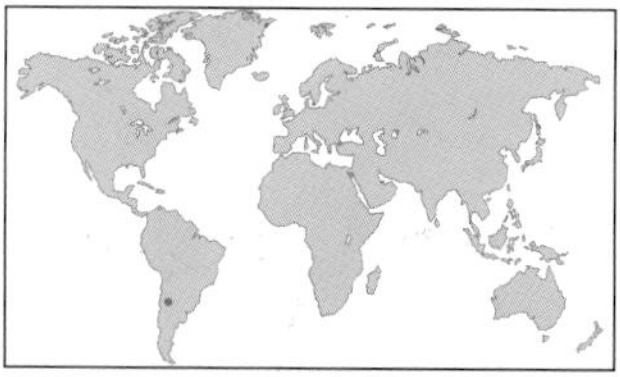

Saltasaurus

(lizard from Salta)

Saltasaurus was a typical Late Cretaceous titanosaurid. These sauropods were the dominant large herbivores of the time in most parts of the world, except North America and Asia.

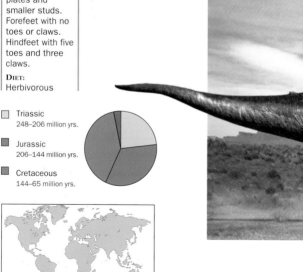

Titanosaurids can be recognized by their unusual ball and socket joints between their tail vertebrae. Despite their abundance, titanosaurid fossils are frustratingly incomplete. Their relationships have been obscure, partly because they display a mix of *Diplodocus*-like and *Brachiosaurus*-like features.

It now seems likely that they were relatives of *Brachiosaurus* (see pp. 64–65), which developed some convergences with diplodocids (such as peg-like teeth). Titanosaurids were quite variable and some were among the largest of land animals, while others were the smallest of all sauropods. While some had armored skin, others did not. *Saltasaurus* was small with a heavily armored, wide body. Its back and sides were covered in small, rounded studs, with scattered larger keeled plates (approximately 4 in [10 cm] in diameter).

ID FACT FILE

LENGTH:
24½ ft (7.5 m)

WEIGHT:
1 ton

TIME:
Late Cretaceous

CLASSIFICATION:
Saurischia
Theropoda
Ceratosauria

DESCRIPTION:
Large, but slender biped. Head short and deep. Large triangular horn over each eye. Short thick neck. Tiny arms with very short forearm. Hand with three stubby fingers and a spike. Long legs with three large toes and a reduced inner toe. Long, thick flexible tail.

DIET:
Carnivorous

Triassic
248–206 million yrs.

Jurassic
206–144 million yrs.

Cretaceous
144–65 million yrs.

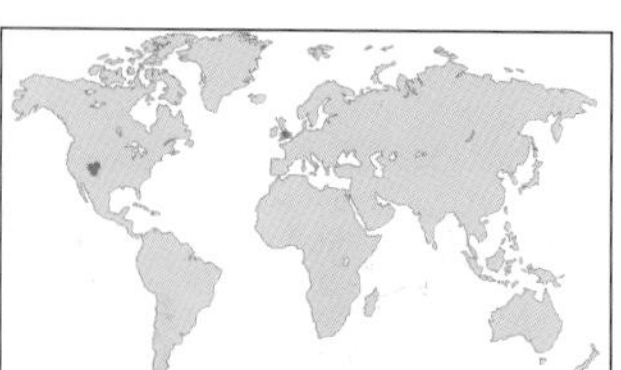

Carnotaurus

(flesh [-eating] bull)

This unusual looking theropod is perhaps the best-preserved member of the recently recognized abelisaurid family. As dinosaur exploration outside of North America improves, we are realizing that abelisaurids were the dominant large carnivores of the latest Cretaceous in South America, Africa, Madagascar, India, and maybe even Europe. Abelisaurids are characterized by their unusual vertebrae and their short snouts.

Other unusual features of *Carnotaurus* are the two stout horns above its eyes and the extreme reduction of the arm bones below the elbow. These are so short as to give the appearance that the hand grew straight out of the elbow without any forearm at all!

The hand also bore a large spike, somewhat like the thumbspike of *Iguanodon* (see pp. 156–157). The skeleton of *Carnotaurus* was preserved with skin impressions showing that it was covered with small round scales and larger conical studs.

ID FACT FILE

Length:
30 ft (9 m)

Time:
Late Cretaceous

Classification:
Saurischia
Theropoda
Ceratosauria

Description:
Like *Carnotaurus* but with a tall bump between the eyes and no horns.

Diet:
Carnivorous

Majungatholus

(dome from Majunga)

The first known fossil of this dinosaur was just a piece of skull roof found on the island of Madagascar. It was very thick and bulged upwards into a tall mound-like structure that closely resembled the domes that adorned the heads of pachycephalosaurs, and so it was classified as one. But that made it a fossil out of place because all other domed pachycephalosaur fossils are from the Late Cretaceous of North America and Asia.

Triassic
248–206 million yrs.

Jurassic
206–144 million yrs.

Cretaceous
144–65 million yrs.

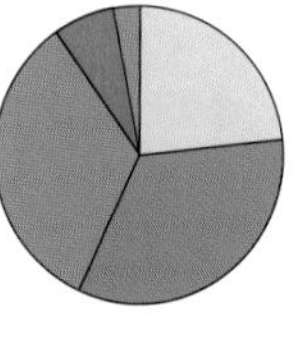

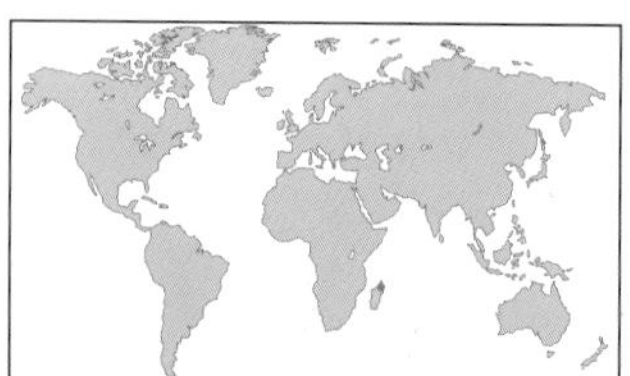

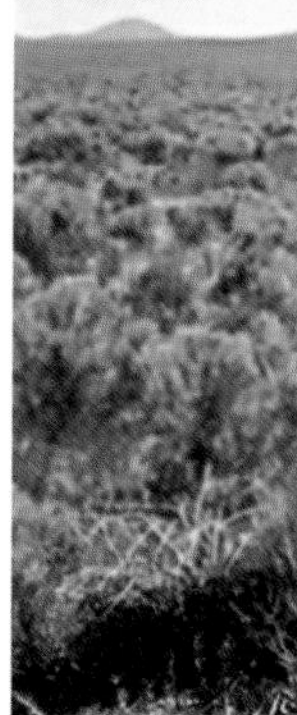

Majungatholus implied that this group was widespread in the Jurassic before the northern and southern continents had separated. However, no scrap of these Jurassic pachycephalosaurs had ever been found. The puzzle was solved when a complete skull was found. It turned out that the "dome" was actually a short, stout horn growing out of a much larger theropod skull. *Majungatholus* was a close relative of *Carnotaurus* (see pp. 180–181), and like it, had a deep head with a short snout.

ID FACT FILE

LENGTH:
36 ft (11 m)

WEIGHT:
4 tons

TIME:
Early Cretaceous

CLASSIFICATION:
Saurischia
Theropoda
Tetanurae

DESCRIPTION:
Large heavy-bodied biped. Head long and low. Tip of jaws expanded. Small central crest on snot in front of eyes. Low ridge on the back, over the hips. Arms large and thick. Three fingers with sharp claws. Thumbclaw very large. Three large toes and a reduced inner toe on feet.

DIET:
Carnivorous, fish

Baryonyx

(heavy claw)

The discovery of *Baryonyx* within the limits of Greater London in 1984 demonstrated that there still remains many dinosaurs to be discovered even in such densely inhabited and thoroughly searched places as England.

The first bone to be found was a very large curved claw, which suggested that the animal could have been a giant dromaeosaurid (eg. *Utahraptor*, see pp. 218–219).

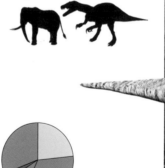

Triassic
248–206 million yrs.

Jurassic
206–144 million yrs.

Cretaceous
144–65 million yrs.

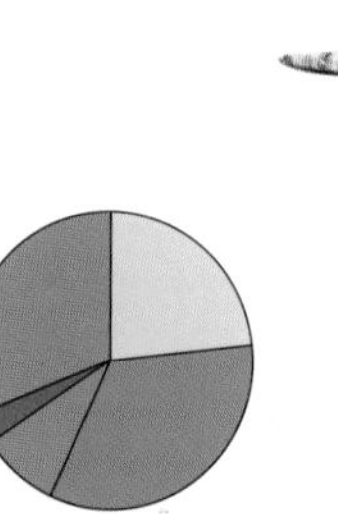

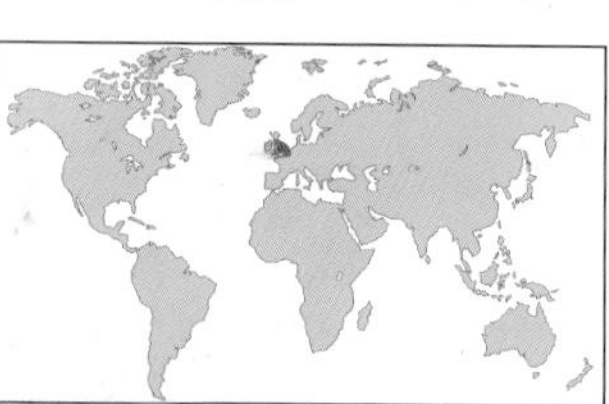

However, it turned out to be the thumb claw of an animal quite unlike any dromaeosaurid. The skull was long and low with an expanded tip (reminiscent of a crocodile), and the lower jaws were crowded with twice as many teeth as would be expected in a theropod of similar size.

We now think that *Baryonyx* was part of an unusual family of theropods, the Spinosauridae, which preyed upon fish. The crocodile-like jaws and teeth support the fish-eating hypothesis as does the remains of a large fish found in the stomach region of the skeleton of *Baryonyx*.

ID FACT FILE

LENGTH:
23 ft (7 m)

TIME:
Early Cretaceous

CLASSIFICATION:
Saurischia
Theropoda
Tetanurae

DESCRIPTION:
Long, low head with widely spaced straight teeth. Snout-tip may have had a crest. Body unknown but probably bipedal.

DIET:
Carnivorous, fish

Irritator

(the irritating one)

Irritator received its unusual name when the scientists who were studying it discovered that its odd shape was partly due to the specimen being doctored. The collector of the specimen had used fragments of bone and car body filler to artificially lengthen the snout. This was done to increase the commercial value of the skull.

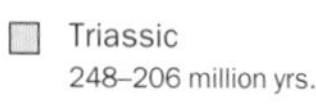

Triassic
248–206 million yrs.

Jurassic
206–144 million yrs.

Cretaceous
144–65 million yrs.

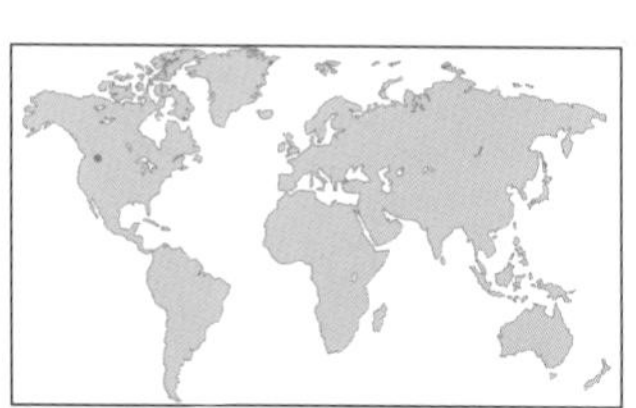

Nevertheless, when the damage was repaired and the fake parts removed, an extraordinary theropod skull remained. Its snout was long and low with widely spaced teeth. These teeth are quite unlike most other theropods because they are straight, circular in cross-section, and lack serrations. The only other theropod known to have teeth like these is the gigantic, but poorly known, *Spinosaurus* from Africa. The skull shape is also similar to other spinosaurids. A spinosaurid snout-tip from the same locality as *Irritator* may belong to this genus; if so, it had a short crest at the front of its snout.

ID FACT FILE

LENGTH:
33 ft (10 m)

WEIGHT:
3.5 tons

TIME:
Early Cretaceous

CLASSIFICATION:
Saurischia
Theropoda
Tetanurae
Carnosauria

DESCRIPTION:
Large heavy-bodied biped. Large deep head and a short thick neck. Low ridges on each side of the dorsal margin of the snout. Arms short. Three fingers with sharp claws. Strong legs with three main toes and a reduced inner toe.

DIET:
Carnivorous, large dinosaurs.

Triassic
248–206 million yrs.

Jurassic
206–144 million yrs.

Cretaceous
144–65 million yrs.

Acrocanthosaurus

(high-spined lizard)

Acrocanthosaurus was the largest terrestrial predator of the Early Cretaceous of North America. It was a carnosaur related to *Allosaurus* (see pp. 80–81). Like *Allosaurus*, it only had three fingers in each hand, an advanced feature evolved convergently with coelurosaurs.

It differed from *Allosaurus* in having a low ridge instead of a triangular horn in front of

each eye. It also had very tall spines on top of each vertebra, producing a tall, thick ridge that ran the full length of the spinal column from behind the head to the end of the tail. The purpose of this ridge is unknown: it may have supported a long, low hump.

Acrocanthosaurus probably preyed upon sauropods. A set of trackways preserved in the famous Palauxy River area of Texas shows a carnosaur (probably *Acrocanthosaurus*) following and attacking a sauropod. Unfortunately, the trackway does not record the conclusion of this encounter.

Charcarodontosaurus

(shark-toothed lizard)

ID FACT FILE

LENGTH:
40 ft (12 m)

WEIGHT:
6 tons

TIME:
Late Cretaceous

CLASSIFICATION:
Saurischia
Theropoda
Tetanurae
Carnosauria

DESCRIPTION:
Like *Acrocanthosaurus* but without a thick ridge along the neck, back, and tail.

DIET:
Carnivorous, large dinosaurs.

This was the last and among the largest of all carnosaurs. Although carnosaurs were the dominant large predators of the Jurassic and Early Cretaceous, they had died out by the end of the age of dinosaurs, being replaced by tyrannosaurid coelurosaurs in the Northern Hemisphere and abelisaurid ceratosaurs in the Southern Hemisphere.

Although *Charcarodontosaurus* was very big, it is hard to say if it was actually the

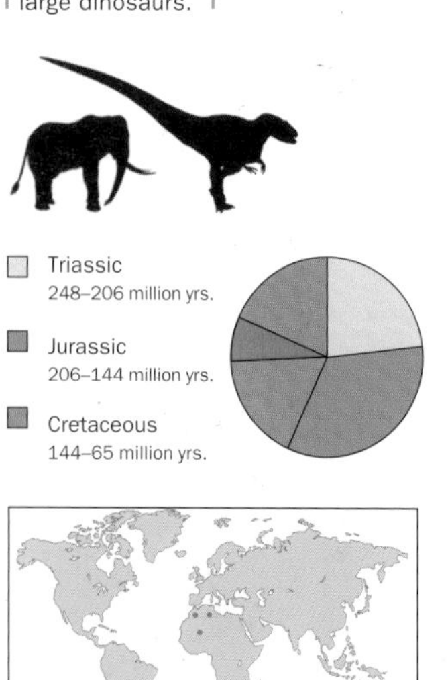

biggest of all carnivorous dinosaurs without more complete remains. A close relative from South America, *Giganotosaurus* and *Tyrannosaurus* also reached a similar size.

It is interesting to recognize that theropods do not seem to have got any larger (as far as we know), so we may be looking at the absolute size limit for a theropod dinosaur. Apart from its larger size, *Charcarodontosaurus* differed from other carnosaurs, like *Allosaurus* (see pp. 80–81), in having a narrower head without small horns in front of the eyes and in having broad, triangular, shark-like teeth.

Alioramus

(other branch)

ID FACT FILE

LENGTH:
20 ft (6 m)

WEIGHT:
1,543 lb (700 kg)

TIME:
Late Cretaceous

CLASSIFICATION:
Saurischia
Theropoda
Coelurosauria

DESCRIPTION:
Medium-sized biped. Large head. Snout with row of six small horns. Small forearms. Number of fingers unknown. Long slander legs. Three large toes and a reduced inner toe.

DIET:
Carnivorous

Alioramus was a primitive member of the tyrannosaurid family. Unlike most coelurosaurs, tyrannosaurids grew very big and preyed on the largest herbivorous dinosaurs in their habitat. Tyrannosaurs became the dominant carnivores of North America and Asia, replacing the carnosaurs and abelisaurids that were the dominant large carnivores elsewhere in the world. Unlike the carnosaurs, they have been confused in the past with tyrannosaurids, who had slender hind legs with proportions designed for fast running.

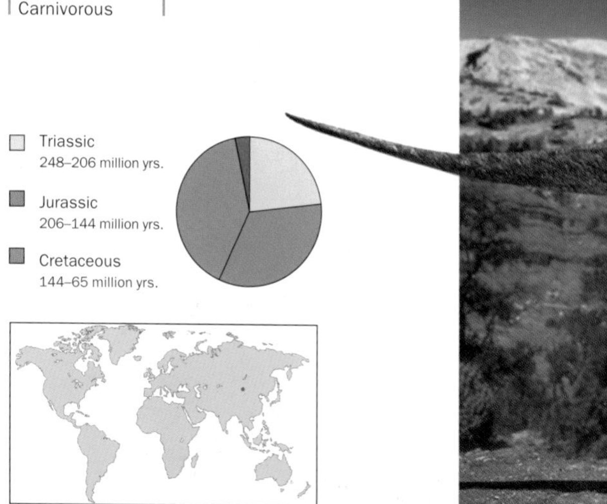

They would have been the fastest animals alive in their size range. Later, tyrannosaurids developed deep, heavily-built skulls whereas *Alioramus* had a longer skull with weaker jaws that are more typical of other coelurosaurs.

Alioramus also differed from other tyrannosaurids in having a row of little spikes along its snout. It is not known whether Alioramus had three fingers like its coelurosaurian ancestors or if it had developed the two-fingered hand that characterizes later tyrannosaurids.

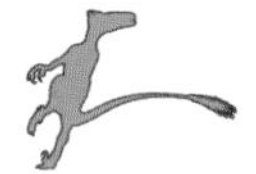

ID FACT FILE

LENGTH:
33 ft (10 m)

WEIGHT:
5 tons

TIME:
Late Cretaceous

CLASSIFICATION:
Saurischia
Theropoda
Tetanurae
Coelurosauria

DESCRIPTION:
Large biped. Head large and deep. Large thick teeth. Neck short and powerful. Arms tiny with only two fingers. Long hind legs with three large toes and a small inner toe. Tail moderately long with a stiff tip.

DIET:
Carnivorous, large dinosaurs.

Tarbosaurus

(alarming lizard)

Tarbosaurus was the Asian equivalent of *Tyrannosaurus* (see pp. 196–197). It is so similar that some argue that it is just a population of *Tyrannosaurus* that was connected to the North American population by a land bridge through the Bering Strait that probably existed in the latest Cretaceous.

Others argue that the similarities are due to convergence and that *Tyrannosaurus* is more closely related to earlier North American tyrannosaurids and that

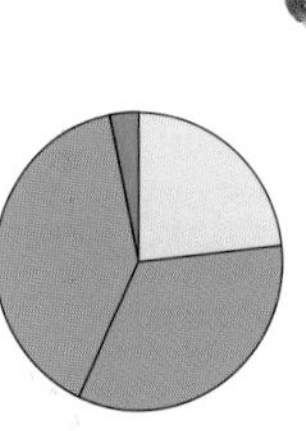

Tarbosaurus is more closely related to other Asian tyrannosaurids, such as Alioramus (see pp. 192–193).

Like *Tyrannosaurus*, *Tarbosaurus* had a large, heavy skull armed with big thick teeth and very reduced arms with only two digits. It differed from *Tyrannosaurus* in having 15 teeth in each lower jaw (versus 13–14 for *Tyrannosaurus*) and in having a skull that was narrower across the cheeks.

Tarbosaurus would have preyed upon the large hadrosaurids, such as *Saurolophus*, that shared its habitat.

ID FACT FILE

LENGTH:
40 ft (12 m)

WEIGHT:
6.7 tons

TIME:
Late Cretaceous

CLASSIFICATION:
Saurischia
Theropoda
Tetanurae
Coelurosauria

DESCRIPTION:
Large biped. Head large and deep. Cheek region broad. Large thick teeth. Neck short and powerful. Arms tiny with only two fingers. Long hind legs with three large toes and small inner toe. Tail moderately long with a stiff tip.

DIET:
Carnivorous, large dinosaurs.

Tyrannosaurus

(tyrant lizard)

This coelurosaur was close to, if not equal in size, to the largest carnosaurs, but had a bulkier build and longer legs. The proportions of the hindlegs are those of a giant running animal. Although its top speed may not have exceeded 25 mph (40 km/h) (a trip or fall at higher speeds would have been fatal for such a giant), it was certainly the fastest animal of its size. It could have easily run down large hadrosaurids and ceratopsians.

Triassic
248–206 million yrs.

Jurassic
206–144 million yrs.

Cretaceous
144–65 million yrs.

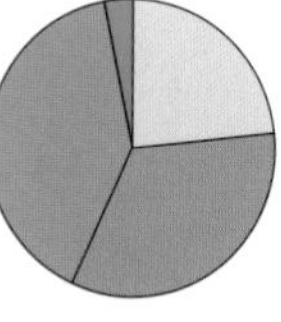

Studies of its teeth have revealed that the design of the serrations on its teeth would have trapped fibers of meat during feeding. These fibers would have provided food for a legion of dangerous bacteria. Thus most animals that escaped an attack from *Tyrannosaurus* would, nevertheless, be killed by a massive infection within days.

CAT scans of its brain cavity reveal that it had an excellent sense of smell that could help it track such dying prey.

ID FACT FILE

Length:
16½ ft (5 m)

Time:
Late Cretaceous

Classification:
Saurischia
Theropoda
Tetanurae
Coelurosauria

Description:
Large biped. Head large and deep. Cheek region broad. Large thick teeth. Neck short and powerful. Arms tiny with only two fingers. Long hind legs with three large toes and small inner toe. Tail moderately long with a stiff tip.

Diet:
Carnivorous, large dinosaurs.

Juvenile Tyrannosaurus

(tyrant lizard)

A small tyrannosaurid skull found in the same strata that produce *Tyrannosaurus* has been described as a pygmy tyrannosaurid, '*Nannotyrannus*'. It was thought to differ from *Tyrannosaurus* in having a longer, more pointed snout and more blade-shaped teeth.

Description of the growth stages of other tyrannosaurid genera has shown that a long pointed snout is a juvenile characteristic. Indeed an examination of the

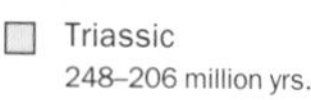

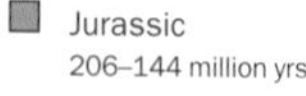

Triassic
248–206 million yrs.

Jurassic
206–144 million yrs.

Cretaceous
144–65 million yrs.

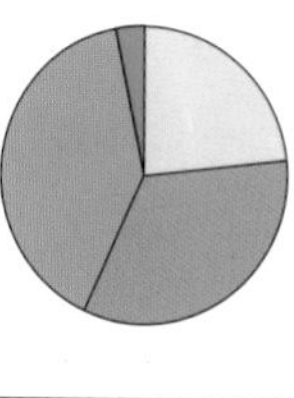

'*Nannotyrannus*' skull has revealed a number of features, such as bone texture, that indicate it is a juvenile. Furthermore, it shares some distinctive characters that are only found in *Tyrannosaurus* such as a broad cheek region and small midline crest on the bones between the eyes (this would not have been visible in life). Thus, most palaeontologist now accept that *Nannotyrannus* is a juvenile *Tyrannosaurus*.

The difference in the teeth suggests that juveniles sliced off meaty parts of a carcass while adults chewed through the whole thing—bones and all.

ID FACT FILE

LENGTH:
6½ ft (2 m)

TIME:
Early Cretaceous

CLASSIFICATION:
Saurischia
Theropoda
Tetanurae
Coelurosauria

DESCRIPTION:
Long, slender neck and small head with pointed beak and a throat pouch. Small fleshy crest behind head. Forearms long. Three equal-sized fingers with long, straight claws. Hindquarters unknown. Skin smooth.

DIET:
Unknown

Pelecanimimus

(pelican mimic)

Pelecanimimus is the earliest known member of the ornithomimid family, which are commonly called the ostrich-mimics. They resemble ostriches in their long, slender necks; small heads with pointed beaks; and long slim legs adapted for fast running. Most ornithomimids lack any teeth, increasing their resemblance to birds. In contrast, *Pelecanimimus* had more teeth than any other theropod.

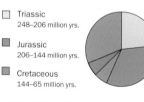

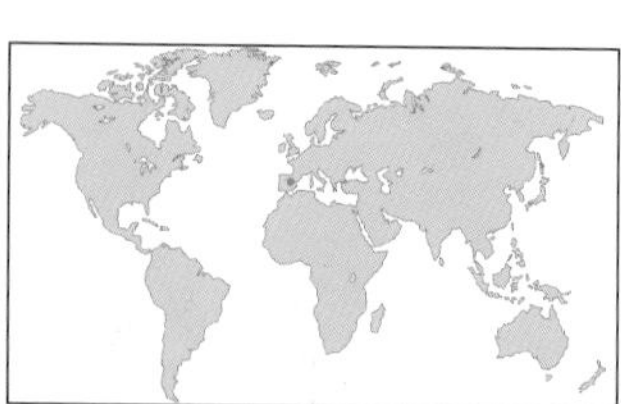

Its teeth were tiny and closely packed so that together they formed a single cutting edge. Perhaps later ornithomimids swapped their teeth for sharp cutting edges on their horny beaks.

Various soft tissues were preserved along with the skeleton of *Pelecanimimus*. These show that there was a small soft crest at the back of the head and that there was a throat pouch, a bit like a pelican's, below its lower jaws. It had a wrinkled, naked skin that lacked both scales and feathers.

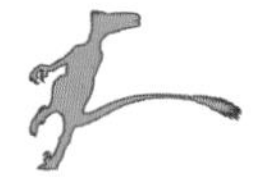

ID FACT FILE

LENGTH:
13 ft (4 m)

WEIGHT:
330 lb (150 kg)

TIME:
Late Cretaceous

CLASSIFICATION:
Saurischia
Theropoda
Tetanurae
Coelurosauria

DESCRIPTION:
Small head. Pointed, toothless beak. Neck long and slender. Compact body. Forearms long. Three equal-sized fingers with long, straight claws. Long legs. Three toes with blunt claws. Moderately long tail with stiff tip.

DIET:
Herbivorous

Triassic
248–206 million yrs.

Jurassic
206–144 million yrs.

Cretaceous
144–65 million yrs.

Struthiomimus

(ostrich mimic)

Struthiomimus was a typical Late Cretaceous ornithomimid. It had small head with a pointed, toothless beak and elongated lower legs that were well adapted for fast running. Like all toothless ornithomimids, it was probably a herbivore.

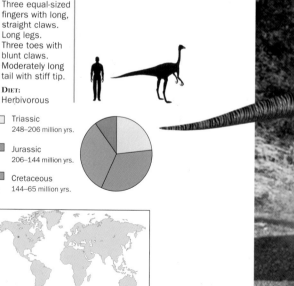

Its forelimbs had many peculiarities that it shared with other members of its family. The claws on its fingers were long and straight, unlike the strongly curved claws of most other theropods. Such claws were not effective for grasping prey.

Another peculiarity was the thumb, which did not oppose the other fingers as it does in most other theropods. Instead, it moved in parallel with the other fingers. This reduced its grasping ability even further but caused the whole, narrow hand to form a hook-like structure when flexed. Perhaps this hook was used to pull down branches of trees so that the animal could browse on them.

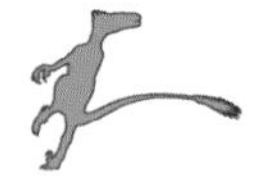

ID FACT FILE

LENGTH:
20 ft (6 m)

WEIGHT:
1,323 lb (600 kg)

TIME:
Late Cretaceous

CLASSIFICATION:
Saurischia
Theropoda
Tetanurae
Coelurosauria

DESCRIPTION:
Same as *Struthiomimus*, only with a blunter snout tip and shorter hands.

DIET:
Herbivorous

Triassic
248–206 million yrs.

Jurassic
206–144 million yrs.

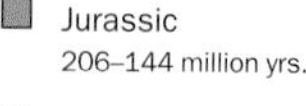

Cretaceous
144–65 million yrs.

Gallimimus

(chicken mimic)

This was a large Asian ornithomimid. It was closely related to *Struthiomimus* (see pp. 202–203) and looked quite similar to it. The main differences were that the beak had a blunter tip and that the hands were shorter. This could have meant that *Gallimimus* had less of a reach and therefore did not browse from tall trees as often as *Struthiomimus* did.

Related ornithomimid remains from China show that they were herbivores that plucked food with their beaks then ground it up in a gizzard filled with grit and small pebbles.

Like other ornithomimids, the foot of *Gallimimus* was adapted to little else but fast running. The inner toe was completely missing and the remaining toes were short and their claws very blunt. Juvenile *Gallimimus* skulls have been found. These had larger eyes and shorter beaks than the adults.

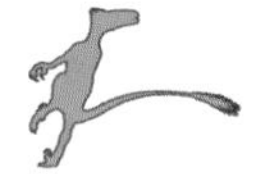

ID FACT FILE

Length:
13 ft (4 m)

Weight:
440 lb (200 kg)

Time:
Early Cretaceous

Classification:
Saurischia
Theropoda
Tetanurae
Coelurosauria

Description:
Heavy bodied biped. Head small and neck long. Arms long. Hand with three fingers each with a large curved claw. Foot with four toes. Tail short.

Diet:
Herbivorous

Triassic
248–206 million yrs.

Jurassic
206–144 million yrs.

Cretaceous
144–65 million yrs.

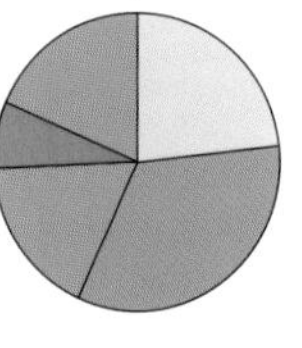

Alxasaurus

(lizard from the Alxa Desert)

The discovery of *Alxasaurus* was like the dinosaurian equivalent of finding the Rosetta Stone because it cleared up a number of mysteries at once. The first puzzle it solved was the proper placement of the weird segnosaurs.

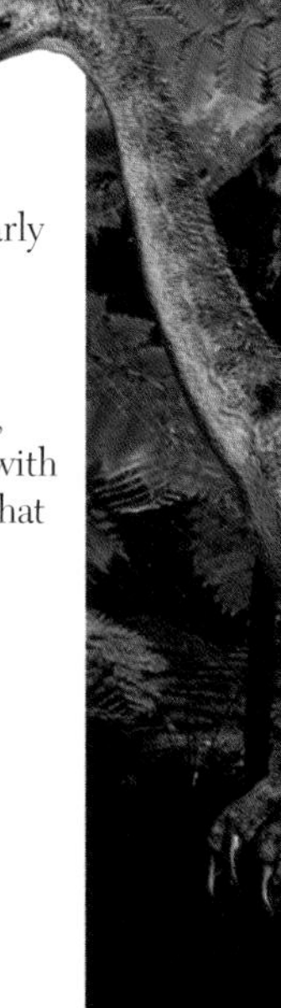

Alxasaurus was clearly a member of this group as it had the same down-turned jaws, leaf-like teeth, and four-toed foot with long straight claws that other segnosaurs had. Segnosaurs were once thought of as late surviving prosauropods or possibly primitive ornithischians. However, *Alxasaurus* was complete enough to show that they were clearly theropods related to *Oviraptor* (see pp. 212–213).

Alxasaurus also showed us for the first time what the skeleton of a segnosaur looked like. They were fat-bodied, large-armed, and short-tailed bipeds. The structure of the hand of *Alxasaurus* also solved the identity of some mystery hands that had been called *Therizinosaurus* (see pp. 208–209). Many similarities between the two, such as the unusually large and straight claws, showed that *Therizinosaurus* was a very large segnosaur.

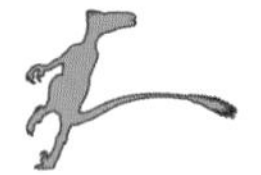

ID FACT FILE

LENGTH:
33 ft (10 m)

TIME:
Late Cretaceous

CLASSIFICATION:
Saurischia
Theropoda
Tetanurae
Coelurosauria

DESCRIPTION:
Heavy bodied biped with very wide hips and abdominal cavity. Three fingered hand with gigantic, straight claws. Four toed foot with long straight claws.

DIET:
Herbivorous

Therizinosaurus

(scythe lizard)

This dinosaur had astonishing sword-like claws on its hands. When these were first found, they were thought to be from some kind of gigantic turtle. Later on their dinosaur affinities were recognized, and later, still, palaeontologists realized that it was a very large segnosaur. None of these later segnosaurs are known from complete remains, so the reconstruction seen here is based on a combination of different large segnosaur parts from the Late Cretaceous.

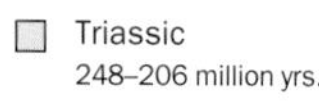

Triassic
248–206 million yrs.

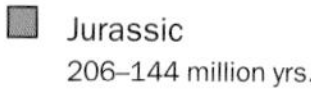

Jurassic
206–144 million yrs.

Cretaceous
144–65 million yrs.

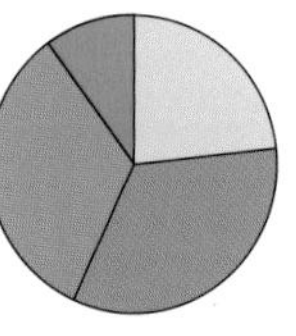

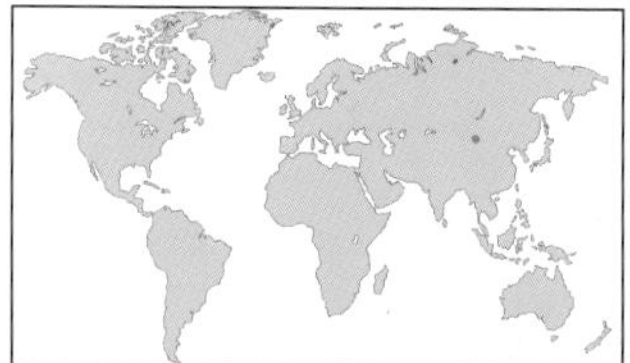

Their hips were broadly flared to support a massive, barrel-shaped gut. Large guts are needed to cope with nutrient-poor plant material. The head was small and ended in a toothless beak. Its hands bore the largest claws of any dinosaur. These claws may have been used in defense, although it has been speculated that they were used to rip open termite nests.

It seems improbable that a multi-ton giant, like *Therizinosaurus*, was able to sustain itself on a diet of ants and termites.

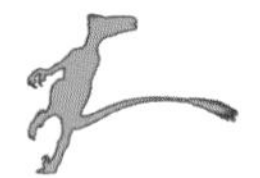

ID FACT FILE

LENGTH:
35 in (10 m)

TIME:
Early Cretaceous

CLASSIFICATION:
Saurischia
Theropoda
Tetanurae
Coelurosauria

DESCRIPTION:
Small, short skull with down turned jaw tips. Small cluster of teeth at the front of upper jaw. Neck long and slender. Short arm with three-fingered hand. Long legs with three main toes and reduced first toe. Very short tail. Body covered with downy feathers. Arms and tail with fans of long feathers.

DIET:
Herbivorous

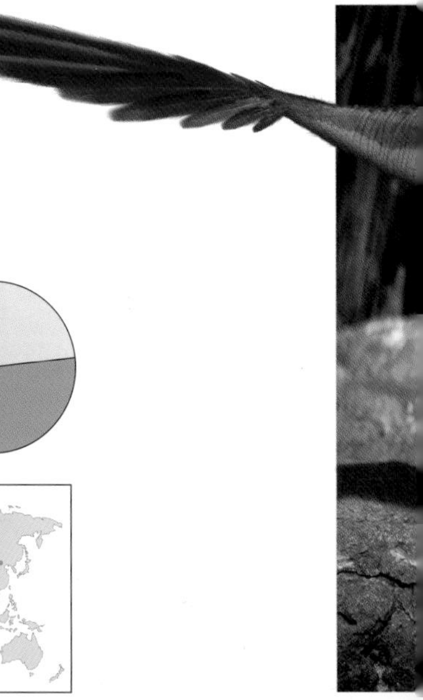

Triassic
248–206 million yrs.

Jurassic
206–144 million yrs.

Cretaceous
144–65 million yrs.

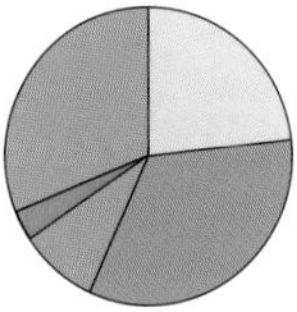

Caudipteryx

(tail feather)

This animal provided the final clinching evidence that has more or less settled the question of origin of the birds. It was a small theropod related to the oviraptorids, and was preserved with unquestionable feathers.

Fans of feathers grew from the second finger of the hand and from the tip of the tail. This was the first time that true feathers had been found with the skeleton of non-bird.

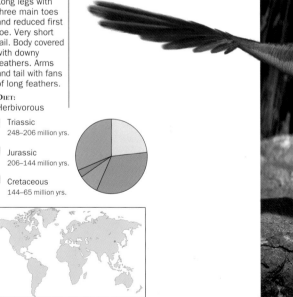

There are some palaeontologists who contend that it is a true, flightless bird. Nevertheless, the close similarities between *Caudipteryx* and oviraptorids make this hypothesis unlikely.

Like oviraptorids, *Caudipteryx* has a short, deep skull, a toothless lower jaw with a bent-down tip, and a very short tail. Unlike true oviraptorids, however, it retained four small, pointed teeth at the front of the upper jaws. Its "wings" were far too small for flight, so they may have been used for display.

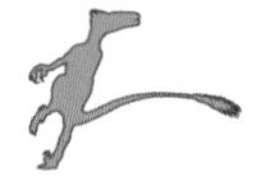

ID FACT FILE

LENGTH:
8 ft (2.5 m)

WEIGHT:
77 lb (35 kg)

TIME:
Late Cretaceous

CLASSIFICATION:
Saurischia
Theropoda
Tetanurae
Coelurosauria

DESCRIPTION:
Large, deep head decorated with a tall crest. Jaws toothless with a horny beak. Long arms. Hand with three grasping fingers and curved claws. Hind foot with three main toes and a reduced first toe. Probably with feathers.

DIET:
Herbivorous

Oviraptor

(egg thief)

Oviraptor was easily one of the strangest theropods. Its toothless lower jaw had an unusual joint with the upper jaw that allowed it to slide back and forth. The upper jaws were also toothless, except for two bony projections arising from the middle of the roof of the mouth.

All these features indicate that it had a highly specialized diet

Triassic
248–206 million yrs.

Jurassic
206–144 million yrs.

Cretaceous
144–65 million yrs.

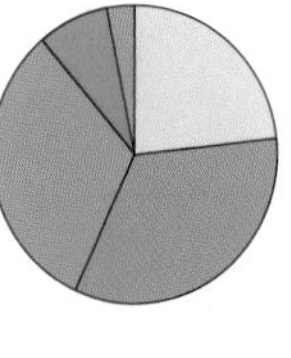

and feeding mechanism. Unfortunately, we have little idea what this diet might have been. Its name suggests that it subsisted on a diet of other dinosaur's eggs. This was because the first skeleton was found lying on top of a nest of eggs. These eggs were once thought to belong to *Protoceratops* (see pp. 134–135), but since the discovery of an embryonic skeleton inside one of them, we know that they are Oviraptor's own eggs. Its seems that the skeleton was that of the mother that died trying to protect her nest from the oncoming sandslide that buried it.

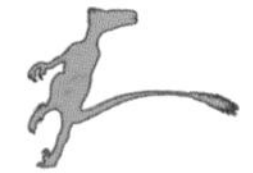

ID FACT FILE

LENGTH:
6 ft (1.8 m)

TIME:
Late Cretaceous

CLASSIFICATION:
Saurischia
Theropoda
Tetanurae
Coelurosauria

DESCRIPTION:
Large, deep head. Jaws toothless with a horny beak. Long arms. Hand with three stout fingers. First finger (thumb) is the largest. Hind foot with three main toes and a reduced first toe. Tail very short. Probably with feathers.

DIET:
Herbivorous

Ingenia

(from Ingen-[Khobur])

Ingenia was a close relative of *Oviraptor* (see pp. 212–213) and would have looked a lot like it but for two differences. The immediately obvious difference is that it lacked the tall head crest that adorned *Oviraptor*. The other difference lies in the hand. In *Oviraptor* the digits were long (with the middle finger being the longest) and adapted for grasping whereas those of *Ingenia* were short and stubby.

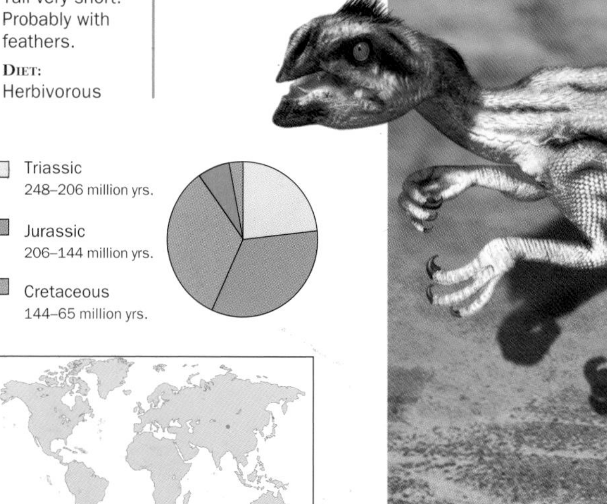

The thumb was the longest and thickest digit of the hand and bore a stout claw. The thumb of *Ingenia* resembled the enlarged thumb of some prosauropods, such as *Massospondylus* (see pp. 48–49), and, like these dinosaurs, probably used it as a defensive weapon. *Ingenia* had the same strange jaw specializations as *Oviraptor* and so would have had a similar diet, whatever it was.

Some type of herbivory is possible given that the related *Caudipteryx* (see pp. 210–211) had a stone-filled gizzard for breaking down plant material.

ID FACT FILE

LENGTH:
11½ ft (3.5 m)

WEIGHT:
110 lb (50 kg)

TIME:
Late Cretaceous

CLASSIFICATION:
Saurischia
Theropoda
Tetanurae
Coelurosauria

DESCRIPTION:
Small, lightly built biped. Long low head. Moderately long neck. Long arms and hands. Three fingers with sharp claws. Long, slender hindlimbs. Foot with sharp curved claw on second toe.

DIET:
Carnivorous, small vertebrates, mammals.

Troodon

(wounding tooth)

Troodon was one of the first North American dinosaurs to receive a name. At the time, only isolated teeth were known. When other parts were found, they were given a different name. It took many decades to match the teeth to the correct skeleton.

Troodon had one of the largest brains of any dinosaur. It also had large eyes and a narrow snout filled with small, curved, and coarsely serrated teeth, possibly

Triassic
248–206 million yrs.

Jurassic
206–144 million yrs.

Cretaceous
144–65 million yrs.

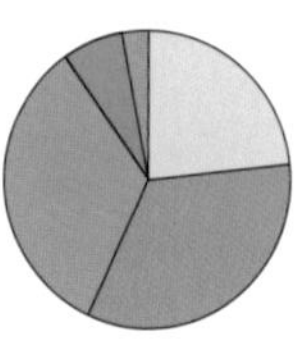

adaptations for preying on mammals. The foot had a large sickle-shaped claw on its second toe that could be lifted off the ground while walking. This resembled a smaller version of the sickle-claw of dromaeosaurids (eg. *Deinonychus* and *Velociraptor* see pp. 218–225), and suggests that *Troodon* may be related to this family.

A *Troodon* has been found buried on top of a nest of eggs containing *Troodon* embryos, which indicates some parental care took place after the eggs were laid.

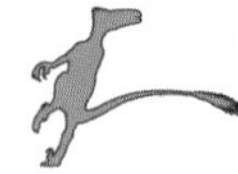

ID FACT FILE

LENGTH:
20 ft (6 m)

WEIGHT:
1,543 lb (700 kg)

TIME:
Early Cretaceous

CLASSIFICATION:
Saurischia
Theropoda
Tetanurae
Coelurosauria

DESCRIPTION:
Medium-sized heavily built biped. Large deep head. Long arms. Hands with large blade-like claws. Relatively short, robust hindlegs. Second toe with very large, sharp curved claw. Long stiff tail. Probably with feathers.

DIET:
Carnivorous, other dinosaurs.

Utahraptor

(Utah thief)

Utahraptor was among the biggest of all dromaeosaurids, the well-known theropod family that are often (and incorrectly) called "raptors."

A distinctive feature of dromaeosaurids was their giant sickle-shaped claw that grew on the second toe of their feet. This claw was needle sharp at its tip and had a blade-like lower edge. The second toe was designed so that the claw could be pulled up off the ground while walking so that it remained sharp.

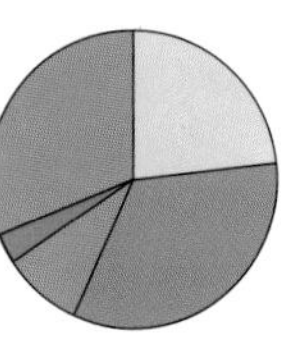

Triassic
248–206 million yrs.

Jurassic
206–144 million yrs.

Cretaceous
144–65 million yrs.

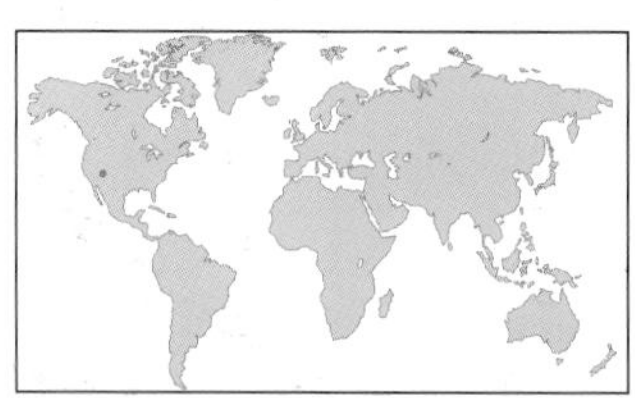

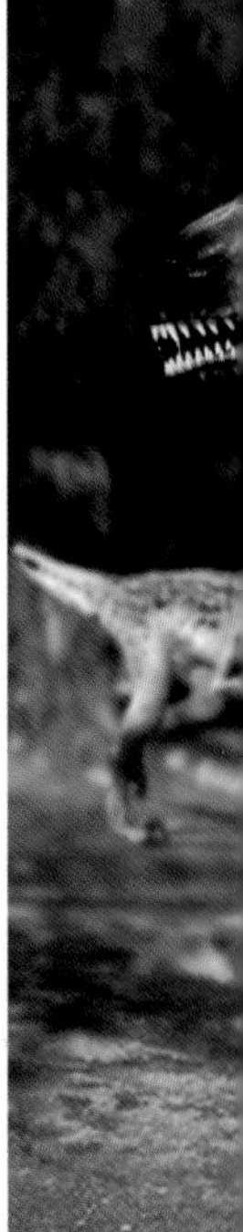

There is no doubt that such a fearsome weapon was used to dispatch prey, possibly using slashing kicks. The hand claws of *Utahraptor* were proportionately bigger and more blade-like than in other dromaeosaurids, suggesting that they also played a big role in making a kill. *Utahraptor* lived at about the same time as the tiny *Microraptor* (see pp. 220–221), indicating that the family had already diversified greatly by this stage and hinting at a hidden history going back into the Jurassic.

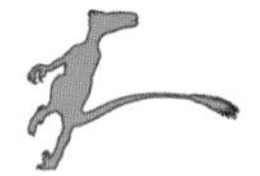

ID FACT FILE

LENGTH:
18 in (45 cm)

WEIGHT:
11 oz (300 g)

TIME:
Early Cretaceous

CLASSIFICATION:
Saurischia
Theropoda
Tetanurae
Coelurosauria

DESCRIPTION:
Tiny biped. Short, triangular head. Long arms. Slender hindlegs. Four toes with curved sharp claws. Inner toe reduced. Second toe with large claw. Moderately long stiff tail. Body covered in long downy feathers.

DIET:
Carnivorous, insects, small vertebrates.

Triassic
248–206 million yrs.

Jurassic
206–144 million yrs.

Cretaceous
144–65 million yrs.

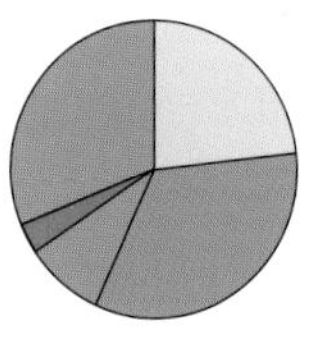

Microraptor

(small thief)

Microraptor is another feathered dinosaur from the Liaoning Province of China. It is also the smallest known adult dinosaur (not including birds, which are also dinosaurs) beating *Compsognathus* (see pp. 82–83), which has held this title for well over 100 years.

Microraptor had a greatly enlarged, sickle-shaped claw on the second toe of the foot and an inflexible tail stiffened by bony rods, as did other members of the Dromaeosauridae.

The enlarged claw could have been used for killing prey or for climbing trees. The other claws were also sharp and strongly curved. It also had digit proportions similar to tree climbing animals. Thus, *Microraptor* would have been more than capable of climbing up into trees (of course we may never know if it really did so).

A dinosaurian origin of the birds need not imply a ground-up origin of flight. Birds could have evolved from a small arboreal coelurosaur like *Microraptor*.

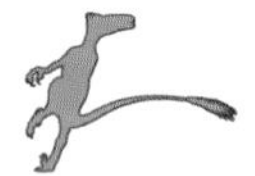

ID FACT FILE

LENGTH:
10 ft (3 m)

WEIGHT:
100 lb (45 kg)

TIME:
Early Cretaceous

CLASSIFICATION:
Saurischia
Theropoda
Tetanurae
Coelurosauria

DESCRIPTION:
Long arms and hands; three fingers with sharp curved claws. Short, robust legs; short second toe with large, retractable claw. Long stiff tail, probably feathered.

DIET:
Carnivorous, other dinosaurs.

Deinonychus

(terrible claw)

Professor John Ostrom's study of this dinosaur in 1969 did more than any other work to spark the "dinosaur renaissance" of the late 20th century.

Previous views painted dinosaurs as slow, cold-blooded creatures that went extinct without leaving any descendants. Yet here was an apparently agile predator. Its tail was stiffened with numerous bony rods so that it formed a counterbalancing rod. The reason it needed such a counter-balance became obvious when the foot was examined.

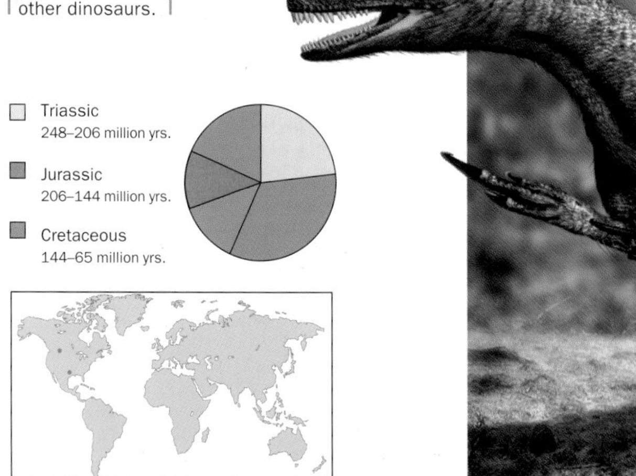

The claw of the second toe had become enlarged into a viciously sharp sickle-shaped weapon. To use this claw the animal would have had to have leapt up onto the animal and delivered a powerful kick, a feat that would require excellent balance.

The other surprise was that many parts of the skeleton of *Deinonychus* were almost bone-for-bone matches with those of *Archaeopteryx* (see pp. 86–87), the earliest known bird. This revived the old idea that birds are the direct descendants of coelurosaurian dinosaurs.

Velociraptor

(fast thief)

This is perhaps the best known of all dromaeosaurids. It is known from many superbly preserved skeletons from the Gobi Desert of Asia. It was a small dromaeosaurid that differed from others in having a long, low head with a distinctive depression in the profile of the snout. It lived in a sandy desert along with *Oviraptor* (see pp. 212–213) and *Protoceratops* (see pp. 134–135).

ID FACT FILE

LENGTH:
6½ ft (2 m)

WEIGHT:
33 lb (15 kg)

TIME:
Late Cretaceous

CLASSIFICATION:
Saurischia
Theropoda
Tetanurae
Coelurosauria

DESCRIPTION:
Like *Deinonychus* but head lower profile of snout depressed between nostrils and eyes

DIET:
Carnivorous, small dinosaurs, and other vertebrates.

Triassic
248–206 million yrs.

Jurassic
206–144 million yrs.

Cretaceous
144–65 million yrs.

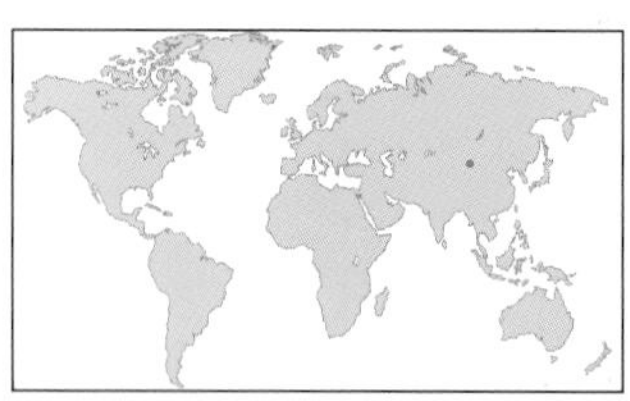

Protoceratops may have been its main prey; the skeleton of a *Velociraptor* has been found locked in what appears to be a fatal struggle with a *Protoceratops*.

Like other dromaeosaurids, *Velociraptor* shows many bird-like details in its skeleton, such as a furcula (wishbone) in the shoulder girdle, large half-moon shaped bone in the wrist, and a backswept pubic bone (the "bird-hipped" condition). The proportions of the digits of the hands also match those of *Archaeopteryx* closely.

ID FACT FILE

LENGTH:
6½ ft (2 m)

TIME:
Late Cretaceous

CLASSIFICATION:
Saurischia
Theropoda
Tetanurae
Coelurosauria
Aves

DESCRIPTION:
Large bird. Long, low head with toothed beak. Long neck. Tiny, rudimentary wings. Splayed hind legs placed far back on body. Four toes, outer toes larger than inner toes. Tail reduced to a stump.

DIET:
Fish

Hesperornis

(single crested lizard)

Hesperornis was an early toothed bird. It had given up its powers of flight to become an aquatic fish hunter, much like the modern penguin. It was so adapted for this mode of life that its wings had reduced to tiny splints of bone, and it could no longer walk upright on land. Instead, it would have to push itself along on its belly. This was because the legs were placed very far back along the long body and stuck out sideways to gain

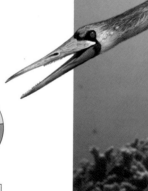

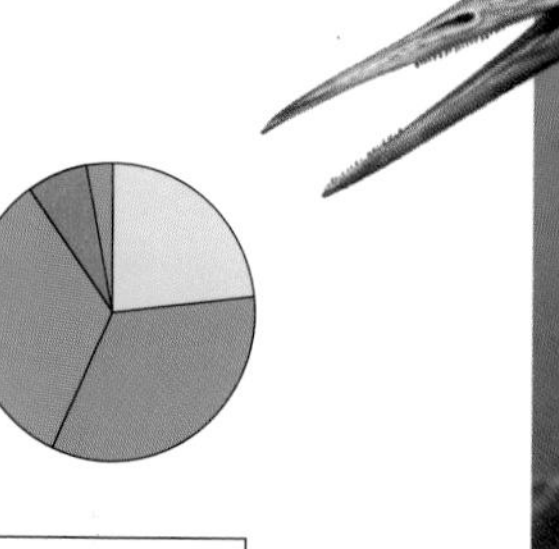

maximum propulsion from the kicks of its powerful webbed feet.

Like modern diving birds, it has all of its toes rotated to point forwards. Its bones have been found in marine rocks that were hundreds, if not thousands, of miles from the nearest shoreline. Obviously this bird was used to travelling far out to sea. It probably spent most of its life at sea, returning to shore only to breed.

Ichthyornis

(fish bird)

ID FACT FILE

LENGTH:
8 in (20 cm)

TIME:
Late Cretaceous

CLASSIFICATION:
Saurischia
Theropoda
Tetanurae
Coelurosauria
Aves

DESCRIPTION:
Medium-sized bird. Long, toothed beak. Moderately long neck. Clawless wings. Broad paddle-like feet. Tail reduced to stump, probably supporting a fan of feathers.

DIET:
Fish

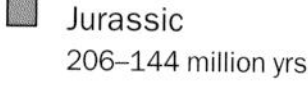

Triassic 248–206 million yrs.

Jurassic 206–144 million yrs.

Cretaceous 144–65 million yrs.

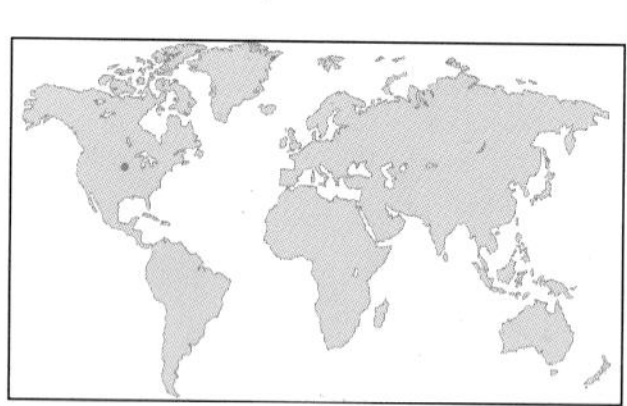

Ichthyornis fossils have been found alongside those of *Hesperornis* (see pp. 226–227), so it too was no stranger to the open sea. However, unlike *Hesperornis*, it could fly. It had well-developed wings and a deeply keeled breastbone for the attachment of flight muscles. Despite the rather modern appearance of its flight apparatus, it still retained teeth in

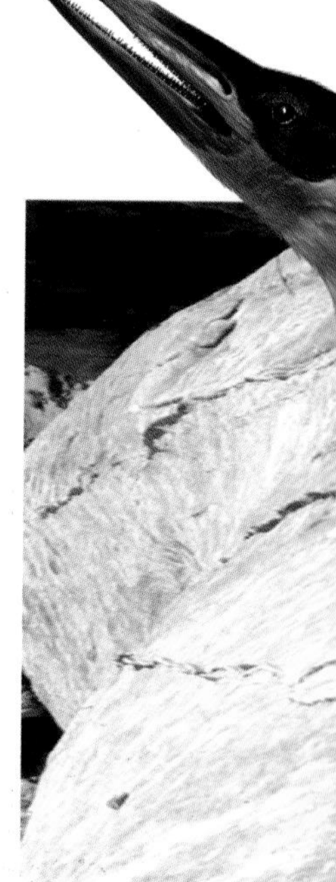

its jaws. These teeth were small, curved and sharp and would have been very useful for holding onto slippery prey.

When it was first found, the idea of a toothed bird was so bizarre that the jaws were identified as belonging to a small marine lizard, despite the fact they were found together with the rest of the *Ichthyornis* skeleton. We now know that those jaws really did belong to *Ichthyornis*. It probably lived like a modern tern or gull, flying out to sea and plucking small fish from the surface of the water.

Koolasuchus

(Kool's crocodile)

ID FACT FILE

LENGTH:
8 ft (2.5 m)

TIME:
Early Cretaceous

CLASSIFICATION:
Amphibia, Temnospondyli

DESCRIPTION:
Large, sprawling quadruped. Large, flattened, semicircular head. Eyes directed upwards. Mouth with two rows of sharp teeth and several pairs of fangs. Short limbs, forefoot with four toes, hindfoot with five. Tail shorter than body.

DIET:
Carnivorous, mostly fish.

Koolasuchus is the last known member of the temnospondyls, a large group of amphibians that dominated the waterways of the world long before the dinosaurs evolved.

Most temnospondyls died out at the end of the Triassic, but a few relatives of *Koolasuchus* survived past this boundary. *Koolasuchus* may have been able to survive for so long because it lived close to the South Pole, as did *Laellynasaura* (see pp. 150–151).

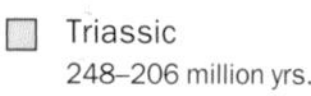

Triassic
248–206 million yrs.

Jurassic
206–144 million yrs.

Cretaceous
144–65 million yrs.

Competitors such as crocodiles may not have been able to withstand the polar winters.

Koolasuchus was an aquatic animal as shown by the weak nature of its limb joints and vertebral column and the presence of a sensory canal system (like the lateral lines of a fish) impressed upon the bones of its skull. It was a predator that probably fed largely on fish; it was capable of taking a small dinosaur while it drank at the water's edge.

ID FACT FILE

LENGTH:
36 ft (11 m)

TIME:
Late Cretaceous

CLASSIFICATION:
Reptilia
Diapsida
Plesiosauria

DESCRIPTION:
Large marine reptile. Head tiny with short snout. Very long interlocking teeth. Neck longer than the rest of the body; thin and flexible. Short rounded body. Paddle-like limbs. Tail short.

DIET:
Carnivorous, Fish.

Elasmosaurus

(thin-plated reptile)

Elasmosaurus and its relatives represent the extreme end of the long necked plesiosaur body plan. In *Elasmosaurus*, the long, serpentine neck took up more than half the length of the body. These advanced plesiosaurs also reached very large sizes, often exceeding 33 ft (10 m) in length.

Their relatively tiny heads were filled with very long interlocking spiky teeth, ideal for snagging slippery prey such as fish.

Triassic
248–206 million yrs.

Jurassic
206–144 million yrs.

Cretaceous
144–65 million yrs.

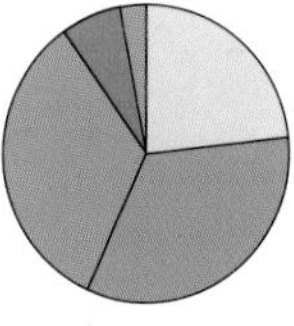

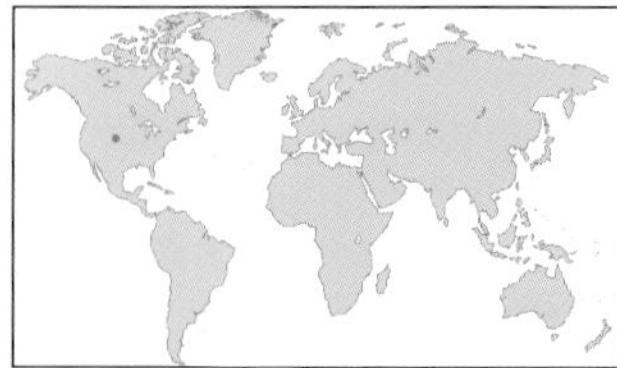

The paddles of *Elasmosaurus* were proportionately smaller than in other plesiosaurs, suggesting that it was a slower swimmer and relying on stealth rather than outright speed to capture its prey.

It may well have positioned itself near schools of fish, thrusting its small head into the middle of it and plucking prey with quick movements of its light head and flexible neck. This would result in a big catch with minimal effort.

ID FACT FILE

Length:
33 ft (10 m)

Time:
Early Cretaceous

Classification:
Reptilia
Diapsida
Plesiosauria

Description:
Large marine reptile. Long, flat head with triangular snout. Neck short and thick. Body compact. Limbs form long paddles. Tail short.

Diet:
Carnivorous, large fish, other marine reptiles.

Triassic
248–206 million yrs.

Jurassic
206–144 million yrs.

Cretaceous
144–65 million yrs.

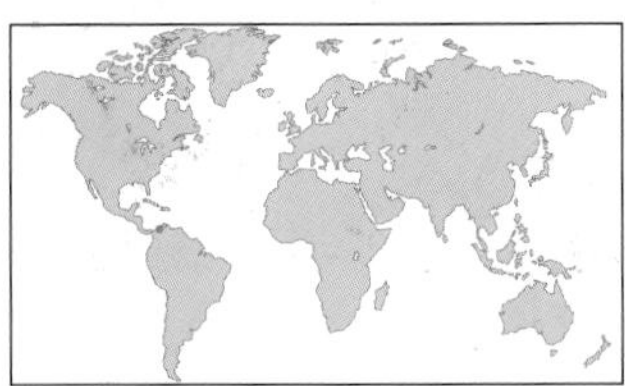

Kronosaurus

(Kronos lizard)

The polycotylids, including *Kronosaurus*, were big headed, short-necked predatory plesiosaurs of the Cretaceous. The length of their skulls exceeded the length of their necks.

They looked a lot like the pliosaurs of the Jurassic (see *Rhomaleosaurus*, pp. 96–97), and are often classified as pliosaurs.

Nevertheless, they share a number of specialized features with elasmosaurids

(eg. *Elasmosaurus* pp. 232–233), such as a reduction in the number of bones of the lower jaw. This indicates that they evolved a pliosaurid like body shape convergently with true pliosaurs.

Kronosaurus was one of the largest of all plesiosaurians. Its huge, flat, head was nearly 10 ft (3 m) long and was filled with pointed teeth the size of bananas. It was clearly a predator that could eat almost anything it came across. Likely prey items included large fish, turtles, and elasmosaurids.

ID FACT FILE

LENGTH:
24 in (60 cm)

TIME:
Early Cretaceous

CLASSIFICATION:
Reptilia, Diapsida
Archosauria
Crurotarsi
Crocodyliformes

DESCRIPTION:
Tiny crocodylian, with a long, flat snout. Several rows of armor plates on its back.

DIET:
Carnivorous, fish, crustaceans , and other small animals.

Bernissartia

(from Bernissart)

Bernissartia was closely related to the ancestors of the modern Crocodylia. Apart from its small adult size, it would have looked little different from a modern broad-snouted crocodile. Nevertheless, it is not included in the group because it lacked certain specialized features of the palate and vertebral column.

The remains of *Bernissartia* were found alongside many complete *Iguanodon*

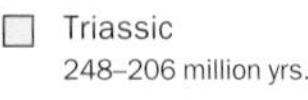

Triassic
248–206 million yrs.

Jurassic
206–144 million yrs.

Cretaceous
144–65 million yrs.

(see pp. 156–157) skeletons in the famous coal mine of Bernissart, Belgium.

Like modern crocodiles, *Bernissartia* would have been an amphibious animal, dwelling in lakes and rivers. Its jaws had pointed teeth at the front for catching and holding fast, slippery prey such as fish. The teeth at the rear of the jaw were thick and blunt and were ideal for crushing hard-shelled prey such as crustaceans.

ID FACT FILE

WINGSPAN:
23 ft (7 m)

WEIGHT:
37 lb (17 kg)

TIME:
Late Cretaceous

CLASSIFICATION:
Reptilia, Diapsida
Archosauria
Ornithodira
Pterosauria
Pterodactyloidea

DESCRIPTION:
Large winged reptile. Almost tail-less. Long narrow wings supported by long fourth finger. Four toes. Head long and low. Jaws pointed and toothless. Long crest projecting back from rear of skull.

DIET:
Carnivorous, fish.

Pteranodon

(winged, without teeth)

Pteranodon is perhaps the most familiar of the large, Late Cretaceous pterosaurs. Its long back-swept head crest produced a very recognizable profile.

Some have suggested that the crest may have acted as a rudder or as a stabilizer for the head during flight, but both of these ideas seem unlikely. Not only were the crests quite variable between individuals (those with very small crests were probably female), but related

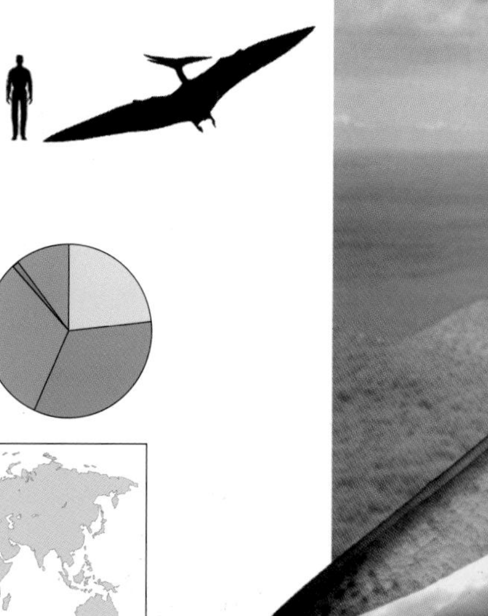

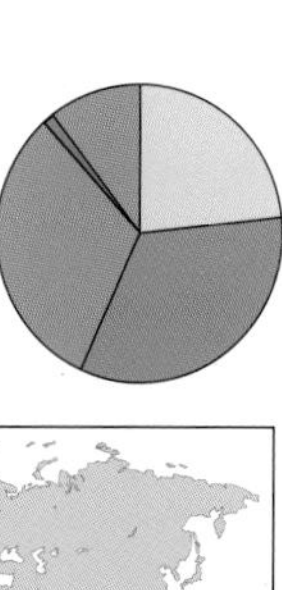

species were able to fly without any crest at all. It seems quite probable that these were display structures used to impress mates and intimidate rivals.

Being that its long, pointed jaws had no teeth, it almost certainly plucked fish from the sea and swallowed them whole. Its remains are found buried in marine deposits that formed many hundreds of miles from the shore, indicating that this pterosaur was used to long ocean flights. It may have spent most of its life at sea, as do some modern seabirds.

ID FACT FILE

WINGSPAN:
13 ft (4 m)

TIME:
Early Cretaceous

CLASSIFICATION:
Reptilia, Diapsida
Archosauria
Ornithodira
Pterosauria
Pterodactyloidea

DESCRIPTION:
Large winged reptile. Almost tail-less. Long, narrow wings supported by long fourth finger. Four toes. Head long and low. Teeth long and sharp. Low crests on upper and lower jaws.

DIET:
Carnivorous, fish.

Anhanguera

(old devil)

The fossils of *Anhanguera* are some of the best pterosaur fossils of all. Not only are its skeletons complete, but the bones have not been crushed flat by the weight of overlying sediments (this usually happens to delicate pterosaur bones). Also, some of its remains include mineralized soft tissues such as patches of skin and wing membrane.

The uncrushed pelvis of *Anhanguera* has helped resolve the debate centered upon the walking posture of pterosaurs. Some have said that they walked erect on their hind feet, while the wings were folded up as modern birds do; others maintain that

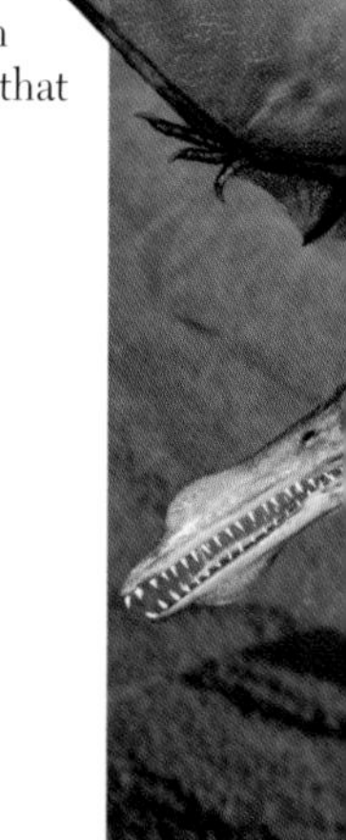

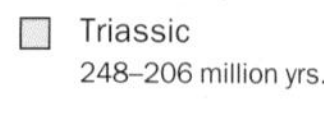

Triassic
248–206 million yrs.

Jurassic
206–144 million yrs.

Cretaceous
144–65 million yrs.

they were quadrupedal sprawlers, like modern bats. The hip sockets of *Anhanguera* show conclusively that it was impossible for it to bring its legs into the erect stance and that the latter model of locomotion must be the correct one.

The low crests above and below the jaw may have helped it cut water while fishing on the wing or may have been used for display.

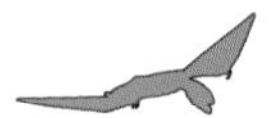

Tapejara

(ancient being)

Tapejarids were pterodactyloid pterosaurs that were closely related to the giant azhdarchid family, which includes *Quetzalcoatlus* (see pp. 244–245). Like them, their small eyes were placed low down on the sides of the head. They also had short, broad wings compared to other pterosaurs with the shoulders placed very low on the flanks, like a modern "bottom-decker" plane. Both of these features suggest that they were slow but highly manoeuvrable fliers.

ID FACT FILE

WINGSPAN:
16½ ft (5 m)

TIME:
Early Cretaceous

CLASSIFICATION:
Reptilia, Diapsida
Archosauria
Ornithodira
Pterosauria
Pterodactyloidea

DESCRIPTION:
Large winged reptile. Almost tail-less. Short broad wings supported by long fourth finger. Head narrow and deep. Toothless pointed jaws. Huge dorsal head crest

DIET:
Carnivorous, fish, and aquatic invertebrates.

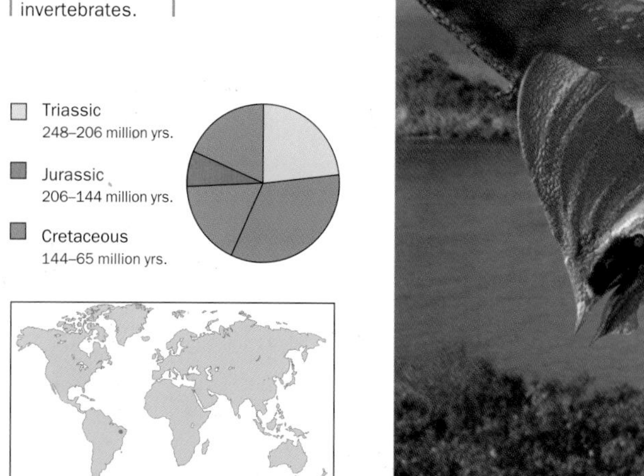

Unlike most pterosaurs, the skull of *Tapejara* was short and deep. The jaws were toothless and the tips protruded as pointed, forceps-like structures. The skull had two bony crests one on top of the head, in front of the eyes, the other projecting backwards from the rear of the head.

We know from spectacularly well preserved fossils that these crests formed the bases for a single, enormous, soft-tissue sail whose height was about three times the length of the skull.

ID FACT FILE

WINGSPAN:
36 ft (11 m)

WEIGHT:
330 lb (150 kg)

TIME:
Late Cretaceous

CLASSIFICATION:
Reptilia, Diapsida
Archosauria
Ornithodira
Pterosauria
Pterodactyloidea

DESCRIPTION:
Giant winged reptile. Almost tail-less. Short broad wings supported by fourth finger. Neck long and stiff. Beak long and toothless. Short crest on top of head.

DIET:
Fish, and other small animals.

Quetzalcoatlus

(named after Quetzalcoatl)

Quetzalcoatlus was among the last of the pterosaurs and was quite possibly the largest flying animal of all time. The largest bones come from an animal the size of a small aeroplane.

Its remains have been found in an inland site that formed on a floodplain, so it seems that the animal did not soar over the open ocean in the manner that *Pteranodon* did (see pp. 238–239).

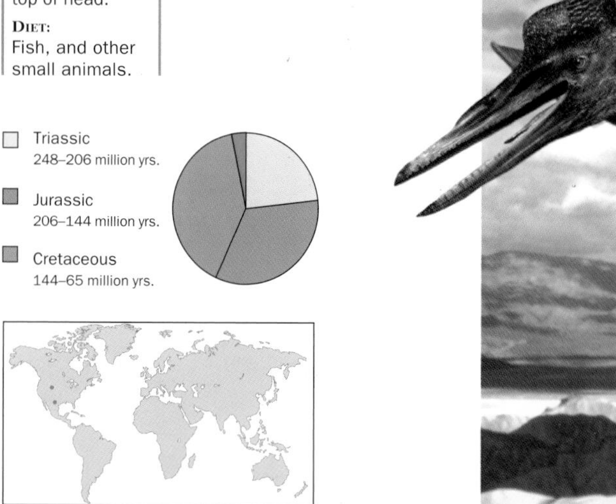

Some people have speculated that the animal lived like a giant vulture, riding thermal updrafts and using its long neck to probe dinosaur carcasses. However, the skull was unknown when this was proposed. We now know that it had a long, straight toothless beak that was inappropriate for tearing carrion off of bones.

Perhaps it was more like a giant stork, wading in shallow water catching fish, frogs, and other small animals. Like many pterosaurs, *Quetzalcoatlus* bore a head crest that was probably used for display.

ID FACT FILE

LENGTH:
14 in (35 cm)

TIME:
Early Cretaceous

CLASSIFICATION:
Synapsida
Therapsida
Mammaliaformes
Mammalia
Monotremata

DESCRIPTION:
Medium-sized mammal. Head probably with short, fleshy bill and simple external ears. Posture probably sprawling. Hind foot probably with sharp spur.

DIET:
Carnivorous, aquatic invertebrates.

Steropodon

(lightening tooth)

Steropodon caused a sensation when it was found in the 1980s. It provided the first unequivocal evidence that mammals inhabited Australia during the Mesozoic Era. Adding to its special status was the nature of the fossil: it was a jaw with teeth that had been completely replaced by opal.

The modern Australian mammal fauna is dominated by marsupials (pouched

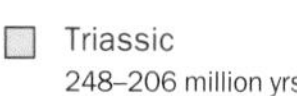

Triassic
248–206 million yrs.

Jurassic
206–144 million yrs.

Cretaceous
144–65 million yrs.

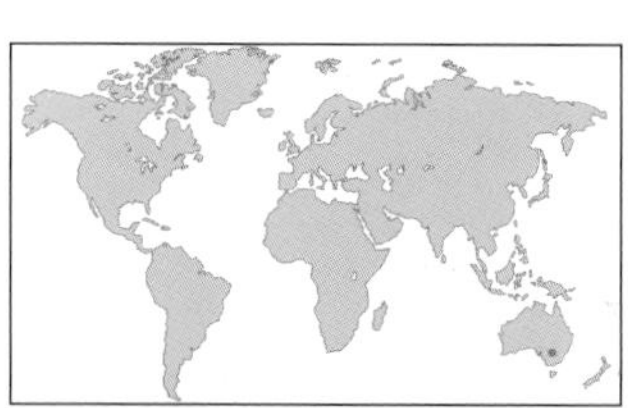

mammals), so everyone was expecting Australian Mesozoic mammals to have been marsupials as well. However, *Steropodon* turned out to be a monotreme closely related to the modern platypus.

Monotremes are an ancient lineage of mammals that lay eggs instead of giving birth to live young. Many more monotremes now have been found in the Mesozoic of Australia, but no marsupials. We now think that marsupials are more recent invaders into Australia that have pushed the monotremes to the very brink of extinction (only three specialized species survive).

ID FACT FILE

LENGTH:
20 in (50 cm)

TIME:
Late Cretaceous

CLASSIFICATION:
Synapsida
Therapsida
Mammaliaformes
Mammalia
Marsupalia

DESCRIPTION:
Medium-sized mammal. Body unknown but probably four-legged. Head probably large with flesh lobes surrounding external ear. Canine teeth large. Fingers and toes probably five.

DIET:
mostly meat, either from small animals or from scavenging.

Didelphodon

(opossum tooth)

Although it is easy to think of Australia as being the home of the marsupials, the marsupials are, in fact, relatively recent invaders of that continent. They may not have reached it until after the Mesozoic Era had finished.

In contrast, North America has a long fossil record of Mesozoic marsupials stretching back to the beginnings of the group and is probably the continent on which marsupials originated. *Didelphodon* was the

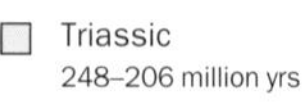

Triassic
248–206 million yrs.

Jurassic
206–144 million yrs.

Cretaceous
144–65 million yrs.

largest of these North American Mesozoic marsupials. Its teeth were more adapted to shearing than its opossum relatives, which tend to be omnivorous. This shearing ability would have helped *Didelphodon* cope with a high meat diet. It may have hunted small animals, scavenged dinosaur carcasses, or both. Like most primitive mammals, it is most likely that *Didelphodon* was nocturnal.

WHAT NEXT?

If after reading this book you feel you would like to know more about the animals described, there are several ways of following up this interest. You can read more about them (see Further Reading pp.10–11), look up one of the many websites on the Internet, visit a museum, or you can join an organization devoted to their study.

Websites

There are many websites dealing with dinosaurs of widely varying quality. Here is a short list of some of the better ones:

The Dinosaur
http://www.ucmp.berkeley.edu/diapsids/dinosaur.html
This is a good introductory page.

Zoom Dinosaurs
http://www.EnchantedLearning.com/subjects/dinosaurs
A good introduction to dinosaurs for children.

Dinosaurs On Line
http://www.dinosauria.com
This page is a good repository of lots of dinosaurian information.

There are several catalogues and databases of dinosaurs. These are three of the best and contain exhaustive lists of known dinosaur genera.

The Dinosauricon
http://www.dinosauricon.com

Dinobase
http://www.palaeo.gly.bris.ac.uk/dinobase/dinopage.html

Dinodata http://www.dinodata.net

For information on any dinosaurian topic you can search the archives of the dinosaur mailing list at:

http://www.cmnh.org/fun/dinosaur-archive/index.html which is a discussion group with contributors that include interested amateurs and professional palaeontologists. This archive will also contain instructions on how to subscribe to this list if you wish to do so.

Other good vertebrate palaeontology sites not directly involved with dinosaurs include the following:

Oceans of Kansas
http://www.oceansofkansas.com
An excellent site covering the varied creatures that lived in and around the seas of the Cretaceous.

The Ichthyosaur Pages
http://www.ucmp.berkeley.edu/people/montani/ichthyo/index.html
A good site with lots of detailed information on the 'fish lizards'.

Museums
The Natural History Museum, Cromwell Road, London

National Museum of Wales, Cathays Park, Cardiff

Royal Scottish Museum, Chambers Street, Edinburgh

National Museum of Ireland, Dublin

The Smithsonian Institution, Constitution Avenue, Washington D.C.

American Museum of Natural History, New York

INDEX OF DINOSAURS

INDEX OF ERAS